The Excellerated Business Success Model

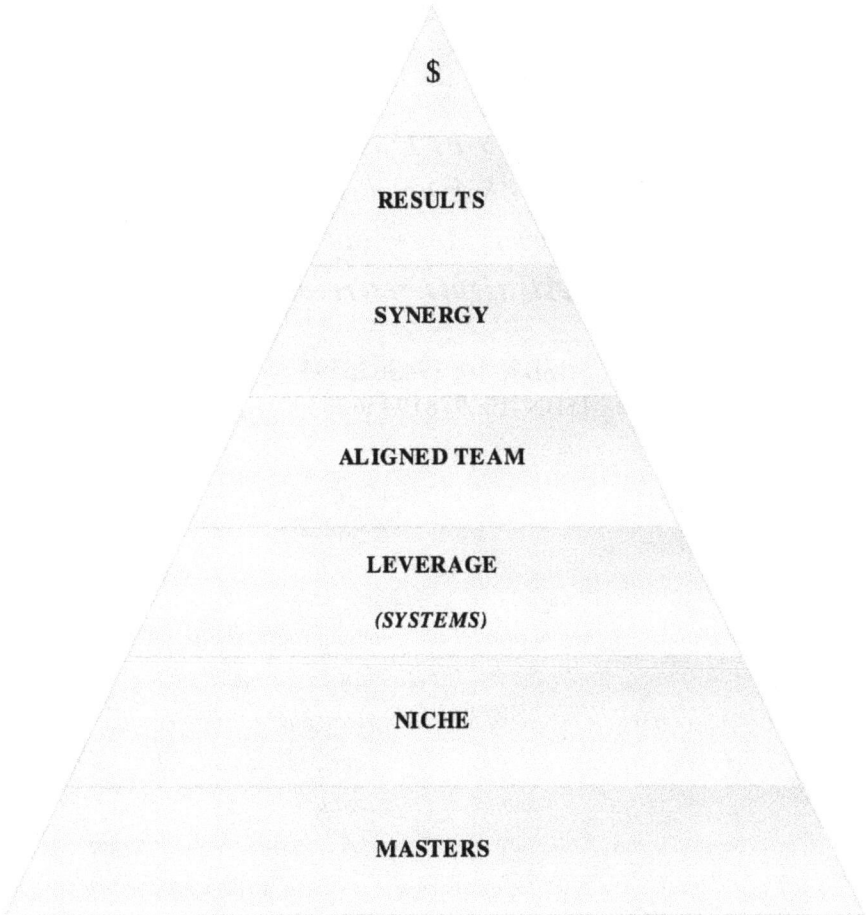

$

RESULTS

SYNERGY

ALIGNED TEAM

LEVERAGE

(SYSTEMS)

NICHE

MASTERS

Published by Waterfront Press
http://waterfrontdigitalpress.com

ISBN-10: 1943625395
ISBN-13: 9781943625390

Dedication

This book is dedicated to all of the graduates and supporters of our programs; the creators of the work; the business partners and associates that for nearly 40 years have financially supported the success of the work; all of the masters that have taught for us – and have provided their wisdom to us personally.

To all that contributed to the success of the work... Thank YOU!

Testimonials About the Work

"In business, it is not task, money or products that make the biggest difference. It's people and relationships. Money & You teaches this. I was so impressed by its effectiveness, I personally sent over 200 people – friends, family, and staff – from The Hour Glass to attend Money & You. And the important tools the program delivered helped me create the platform from which I developed my ideas for sustainable ventures beyond my traditional commercial enterprises."
Dato' Dr. Jannie Chan – Founder, Save Our Planet Investments Pte. Ltd. – Co-Founder, The Hour Glass Ltd.

"Money & You's work in education is powerful, profound and life-changing. I salute their efforts, and I recommend it highly!"
Anthony Robbins, Best Selling Author, Life Performance Master Coach

"Money & You changed my life and redirected my business career. The program is more about discovering ourselves than it is about money, yet in the process, I learned more about money than I ever dreamed possible."
Robert T. Kiyosaki - Best-selling Author, *Rich Dad/Poor Dad* Book Series

"Money & You showed up in Sydney, Australia just at the right time for me. With a broken marriage and a business losing money, I needed a new direction. The generalized principles taught are just that: generalized. They apply in all cases. Once I whipped the courage to implement these principles, my life started to change in a dramatic way. 25 years later, I can put my hand on my heart and say that the significant success I have achieved is due primarily to following these principles in everything I do."
Dominique Lyone – Founder, Managing Director COS (Complete Office Supplies)

iv

"Money & You is one of the most brilliant trainings on the Planet. I took it, learned it, and earned vastly more because of it. You can do the same or more."

Mark Victor Hansen – Co-Author, Chicken Soup for the Soul series, One-Minute Millionaire

"After graduating with honors from UCLA Dental School as a children's dentist, I wanted to make a difference and add value to the world. I faced the daunting task of starting, running and growing my own business. Realizing quickly, I had no knowledge of how to create my dream. Fortunately, I took the Money & You in 1980. At that time, I had one small dental office in Oakland, California producing $350,000 per year. Within two years it grew to nine offices throughout California with a production of over $5 million annually. Through the principles I learned from Money & You, I was able to change the lives of 1000's of people while leveraging myself to explore other passions."

Dr. Jeff Alexander – Founder & Creator Youthful Tooth Co.

"The Money & You Program has allowed me to release and clear many past emotional pains and blocks that no longer serve me. It supported me to become more empowered personally; to harness an abundance of money; to have excellent relationships with my family, business associates, and friends; and to be an even more effective CEO and business leader."

Dame Wendy Tan – CEO, Globe Engineering Sdn Bhd

"I have seen many people attend various financial training events only to do nothing with the information. Why? Because they were missing the Money & You training. It's simply superb and needed by everyone. It's the answer many are seeking without knowing it."

George Antone – Chief Wealth Strategist – Achievest
Creator of *The Family Bank Game*

"As a passionate Social Entrepreneur and a promoter of the For-Benefit-Business Movement, I truly believe Dame DC Cordova and Money & You embody what this movement is all about. Addressing the social issues affecting our world decades before they became acceptable global business topics, DC is a true change-maker in making the world a better place. At the core of her mission is creating more heart-centered business leaders and social entrepreneurs. Money & You is the training ground for that heart awakening."
Haider Nazar – CEO, Achievest

"Before I attended Money & You and the Excellerated Business School for Entrepreneurs, I was scraping by with only $200 dollars a week. And within two years, I had achieved more financially than I had thought possible. I became a millionaire within those two years, earning between $50,000 and $100,000 per month working no more hours per week than the average employee – often much less!
Andrew Barron – CEO, The Timber Barron

"Money & You is much more than a seminar. It is an experience that will live with you and influence you for the rest of your life. The skills you learn are priceless. No matter what success you have achieved, take this course and experience a quantum leap in your ability to manifest your dreams and aspirations."
Joseph Sugarman – Chairman of BluBlocker Corporation – Marketing Legend

"By 30 I was a self-made millionaire, turning a $2000 investment into what is now a multi-million dollar a year company in the Business and Executive Coaching industry. If I were to pinpoint the program that had the most profound impact on making this happen, I would say hands down was Money & You. I would not be the man I am today if it had not been for this incredible program."
Ben Croft – CEO, The WBECS Group

"In the 25 years since I was a participant in Money & You, I have devoted my life to the principles and practices that I learned there. For me, this is the ultimate power of this work...that the principles bring power, freedom of choice, simplicity and connection to every aspect of business and personal commitments. And, there is always more to learn and apply. I have used the technology to start two successful businesses, raise two delightful teenagers and bring fun, energy and intention to every area of life."

Kerry Zurier, MCC – Partner, Accomplishment Coaching
Money & You Instructor

"Money & You is one of the top courses I've ever participated in. Brimming with elegant distinctions, it provided me with a blueprint to take my successful work to unprecedented results, extraordinary beyond all expectations in the New York State Department of Correctional Services where I designed and directed the six-month Shock Incarceration Program which has more than 43,000 graduates, with the lowest documented recidivism rate in the nation which saved the New York taxpayers more than US$1.375 billion."

Dr. Cherie Clark – Co-Founder of Social Synergetics
Director of Shock Incarceration and the Willard Drug Treatment
Campus –New York State Department of Correctional Services

"I have participated in seminars, workshops, and experiential trainings for over three decades. Money & You is the most impactful and transformational program I've ever experienced. The program opened me to a much bigger vision, set of possibilities for how I can make money and grow my ConsciousMillionaire.com platform to reach millions of more people. I realized how I was holding myself back, what I needed to change, and developed a new set of tools that empowered me to breakthrough to a higher level, as an entrepreneur, change-agent, and leader."

J V Crum III, MBA, JD, MS Psy
CEO, ConsciousMillionaire.com

Table of Contents

Introduction

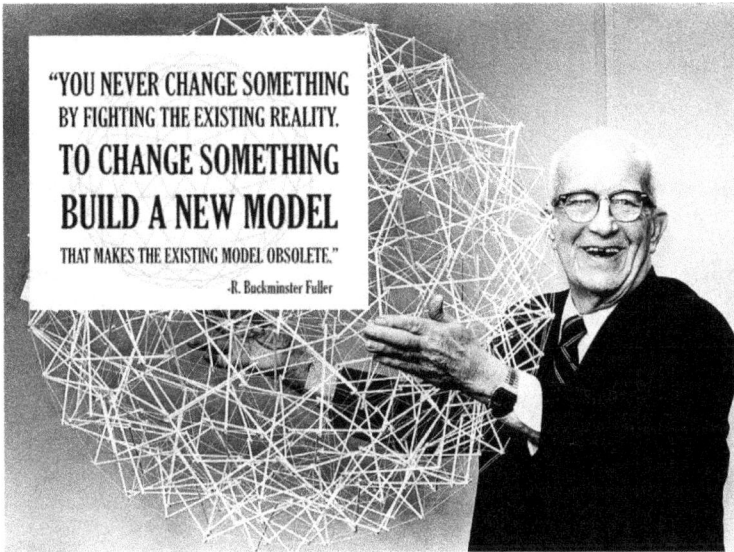

"YOU NEVER CHANGE SOMETHING BY FIGHTING THE EXISTING REALITY. TO CHANGE SOMETHING BUILD A NEW MODEL THAT MAKES THE EXISTING MODEL OBSOLETE."
-R. Buckminster Fuller

The Excellerated Business Success Model

You are about to read about one of the world's most powerful and easy-to-use business formulas... It has been proven effective for decades and can be applied to your business regardless of size, country, location or industry. It works whether you are a for-profit or non-profit. You can apply the steps regardless of your culture, age, or current financial situation.

How do I know this?

My name is Dame DC Cordova, and I've been applying these methods as I have built, grown and lead organizations globally that promote and produce entrepreneurial educational programs. I started this journey after I attended my first business school program back in 1978.

I am also a global business developer for one of the world's leading solar architect and sustainability entrepreneur. This business model is being applied to this emerging renewable energy industry.

It is called the *Excellerated Business Success Model.*

The systems and steps that you will learn in this publication have been tried, tested and proven by world-famous brand-name companies you would instantly recognize and by successful business owners around the world – many that are graduates of our programs!

Once you learn this model, you will start seeing it being applied everywhere.

Of all the principles, systems, and tools that we teach in our programs, it is this *Excellerated Business Success Model* that is the foundation our work. Over 100,000 participants from most industries from over 65 countries have learned, and many have applied it. This is the ultimate "social proof" and the reason why so many graduates come back over and over again to review our programs (they have a lifetime membership). And ultimately this is why they refer their business associates, partners, friends, and relatives to us. Bottom line, it just works!

We've been teaching principles of generating "true wealth" around the globe through our experiential, transformational, entrepreneurial programs since the late 1970's. *Money & You*® and the *Excellerated Business School*® *for Entrepreneurs* programs were designed, and originally led, by the creator, attorney and business consultant, Marshall Thurber. He along with various partners, and later including Bobbi DePorter of http://www.SuperCamp.com put to work many of the principles taught in our *Excellerated* programs in their property development company in San Francisco first and then started teaching them to others through their first *Burklyn Business School for Entrepreneurs,* which I attended.

Later, Robert T. Kiyosaki, co-author of the *Rich Dad/Poor Dad* Series – and my business partner of 9 years – led the programs. Currently, they are being taught by other instructors who are successful entrepreneurs that have proven our models by applying them to their own businesses and organizations. These leaders have a great depth of understanding of what we teach including the *Excellerated Business Success Model.*

Before I explain the model and put each part of its systems into perspective, here is a framework – the contextualization – that may help you relate to and apply it yourself.

You are in luck... it is now popular for organizations to promote *"conscious capitalism"* or be *"socially responsible"* or be a *"values-based"* organization – businesses that are profitable and add value to humanity. The world at large is discovering that these attract more clients and customers, especially the younger professionals. Large companies like *Whole Foods, Zappos, Toms Shoes,* and others, pride themselves in running profitable organizations by tapping into a growing interest in humanitarianism and social responsibility.

You may ask, "How does one run an organization like that?" "Are the tools and practices the same for organizations that are not focused on doing good for humanity?"

The answer is simple but not often explained step-by-step as I have done in this publication. While the organizational tools and practices may be similar, it is the *contextualization, principles,* and *values* that are not.

This *Money & You™ Book Series* is designed to give you those proven tools and principles which are context-rich in the simple "secrets" that have worked for entrepreneurs globally for decades. Business owners learned how to apply the principles underlying the systems and were able to build successful, profitable, and highly *"conscious"* organizations over and over again!

This book will cover the *Excellerated Business Success Model.* Other books in the series such as *Access to Cash* will cover subjects like money. We'll have others that will cover in detail why going green is good business, global entrepreneurship, people skills and other key topics we have found through the decades deserve their own publishing focus. Each volume when carefully studied and the principles applied could be complex, but if you follow the steps recommended, they will support your success!

If profits are your only desire, you may find yourself not attracted to this work. I am going to encourage you and your teams to put these proven systems in place throughout your organization because they can create prosperity, efficiency, productivity and fun in the workplace. They will also support you to lead a life of contribution, compassion and caring for others. Not only for the leader and management, but also for all the players in your business. If you are excited by this possibility and you are interested in attracting a younger crowd to your business, make this book your and your team's guideline!

From the very beginning of the design of our programs one of our favorite mentors was, and still is, R. Buckminster (Bucky) Fuller.

You can learn much more about him at http://www.moneyandyou.com/buckminster-fuller/. He is known by many as the "the planet's friendly genius." He is perhaps one of the best-known American thinkers of the 20th century. He was an architect, mathematician, engineer, author, designer, cosmetologist, scientist, inventor, visionary, and philosopher. He coined the words "synergy" and "Spaceship Earth." He developed the *World Game*. He invented his own mathematics known a Synergetics; created the geodesic dome; and was recognized globally for his creative contributions to technology and the future. He is considered to be the "Leonardo da Vinci" of the 20th century. Many of the principles that we teach in our programs came from his mentorship.

And, ultimately the question that frames the mission we live by was inspired by Bucky…

How do we make the world work for 100% of humanity, in the shortest possible time, through spontaneous cooperation, without ecological offense or disadvantage of anyone?

This mission is no longer a pipe dream. It is an actuality that could occur in as little as two decades. It will be done by entrepreneurs, businesspeople, and leaders who will create organizations that will be inspired to do good, have products that add value to humanity and be profitable!

Soon you'll be able to see why I am inspired to share our principles with you and your teams through these books. The *Excellerated Business Success Model* is a great tool for you to not only share with your employees but also with potential associates, investors, and suppliers. Share it with the interns and independent contractors that work with you. In fact, anyone who does business with you will appreciate knowing about it.

Explain it to those whose success you want to support. It will open conversations about their lives, goals, opinions, and values. They will be able to contribute to your organization and help you define the way you will work together.

That is key when it comes to creating team alignment and support in every area of your business. And when you have it you will create greater bottom-line results. This is true whether you work for-profit or have to raise funds for your non-profit organization.

Systems are at the core of our educational technology because systems (and good management) make the *"invisible visible."* Systems allow you to see what needs to be done next. Systems must be duplicable and self-correcting,

Once a system is established, fine-tuned and well documented, it can then be recreated and duplicated anytime, anywhere. With systems, you are on your way to true freedom! Without them, the best you can have is a business based on the most expensive correction method ever: "trial and error!"

The systems we teach in our programs work powerfully in any field because they are based on proven and tested generalized principles of business and organization. The principles, systems, and tools I will be sharing in this book series are precisely what allowed us to grow steadily, and exponentially through the decades into many different countries. We also grew because so many who have attended our programs have applied the principles successfully in their businesses, organizations (or work) and have created tremendous success.

Many years ago, my good friend Carol Dysart and I compiled an organizational manual entitled *Money-Making Systems – For People Who Work With People*. Popular and sold mainly through our network and Web sites, it was the forerunner of this book series. Carol is an instructor at our *Excellerated Business Schools* and is a people skills expert. She and her associate, Sandra Davis, are key members of our team of experts. They provide personality profiles and coaching to entrepreneurs and our graduates because it is so crucial to hire the right people and run the right systems. Your business results will consistently improve and best of all, they will become predictable! Team alignment becomes easier, conflicts disappear, productivity improves and profits go up!

Plus, it's not necessary for you to be micro-managing everything. This is true *leverage*! This frees you to create new businesses and potentially other profitable endeavors. Or you can study, teach, write, travel (or whatever you wish to do) all the while you keep building your business. You can build it on site or remotely — whatever works for you!

It's mastering the *Excellerated Business Success Model* that has supported me to build, grow, and expand my business while constantly traveling overseas. I bring systems to everything I do, and I work closely with amazing partners, associates, teams, and supporters. Once the systems are set up, I am free to continue to expand the business or move into new industries like renewables.

These tools have given me the ability to choose the life of my dreams while continuing to create multiple streams of income from businesses that produce extraordinary results.

Our organization has flourished globally through our signature programs: *Money & You*® and the *Excellerated Business School*® *for Entrepreneurs*. At first, we grew nationally in the United States from Vermont to Hawaii through 1984.

On July 8th, 1985 the creator of the programs, Marshall Thurber, went on to do other businesses, and I inherited all the rights to the intellectual property of the most transformative, experiential entrepreneurial programs in existence even today.

I, along with my then business partner, Robert Kiyosaki and his wife Kim, were able to take the work internationally, and it grew phenomenally thanks to the work of extraordinary partners, teams and extremely supportive graduates. There was a system for just about everything!

After 9 years of partnership with them, they went on to create the *Rich Dad/Poor Dad* Series with an extraordinary partner, Sharon Lechter, who is a master of publishing, distribution and marketing. She too uses systems to build and grow businesses and to create phenomenal results in publishing, financial literacy educational programs, and being a grand change-maker in high-level policies to transform educational systems and eradicate poverty – totally in alignment with the work that we have been doing for nearly 40 years.

Today we have over 100,000 graduates from over 65 countries – many in the Chinese world through the efforts of our partners http://www.Doers.cn

When you visit www.MoneyandYou.com and review the list of our notable graduates, you will see the names of many industry and thought-leaders; business people, entrepreneurs, best-selling authors, speakers, and training professionals. We are very proud to say that because of them, millions of people around the world have benefited from the principles taught in our *Excellerated* programs.

When people work together as they learn to do with this model, global and local communities of like-minded entrepreneurs are created. They not only want to have profitable organizations, but they also want to add value to humanity...

The result: a celebration of the human spirit that transcends time and space. When people apply these systems, a context of win/win is created; integrity reigns – and the sharing and application of these systems will leave a positive, lasting impression locally and globally for generations to come!

A reunion with over 1000 of our graduates in the Asia-Pacific region!

Chapter 1

Masters

By the time I had attended my first business school and began to apply what I had learned, I began to appreciate how much I was benefiting from my relationships with Masters. The term "Master" refers to any person who has achieved mastery in his or her field of endeavor and is considered by others to be so. This term goes beyond expertise... Masters have an essence about them that goes beyond just being an expert... I could write a whole book on the subject... and let me explain as briefly as possible as this subject is more important than it appears!

For centuries apprenticeships have been a common way of learning skills and professions. In fact, universities as we know them today were only for the rich – the privileged few. People didn't go to school to develop the skills to practice a trade or profession. They learned from someone that had achieved the status of – and earned the right – to be referred to as a Master.

A Master teaches you the "tricks of the trade" that they have learned from their years of practicing a profession or developing their skills. If you learn from their experiences (and mistakes), they can save you a lot of time and money. They can provide you insights on what to do and what NOT to do – if you are wise enough to listen and learn from them.

Once you have determined your personal gift or interest and are ready to focus your business on that interest, the wisest thing you can do is find a Master who is successfully doing or has done what you would like to do.

You will recognize masters because they will be doing their work excellently. They will know their field comprehensively. Masters look at things in their field from a different point of view than others. There is so much you can learn from them! Learn how to approach them and arrange to work with them either for pay or not. As my old partner used to say, *"sometimes it's not about how much you are going to earn, but about how much you are going to learn.."*

If you are still in the process of discovering what your gift or talent is, one of the things you can do to gain some insight and inspiration is to begin working with a Master in a field that you have an interest in. By working with him or her it can lead you to discover or identify your own life's purpose, and from this perspective, it is much easier to identify a niche and create a business promoting that niche.

Many times Masters are looking for someone to continue their legacy. Often, if you have "paid your dues" by applying the principles that they have taught you, it will encourage them to pass their niche to you. Some brilliant Masters get bored and want to move on to create new artifacts, projects, or businesses, and their niche can become yours – an "inheritance" so to speak – and that's exactly what happened to me...

My Early Masters:

I didn't always know that I was an entrepreneur at heart. I grew up in Santiago, Chile surrounded by two female small business owners in the beauty salon industry, my mother and my favorite childhood auntie, her sister. They actually used a small version of the *Business Success Model* in running their beauty salons.

They had salons where they leveraged their resources and assets by renting space to other hair stylists; renting them equipment, and providing their own home-made materials like shampoo; they even taught others how to become hair stylists. My mother reached a beautiful level of mastery – to the point that she had a waiting list of women who wanted to have their hair done by her. And my auntie expanded to other businesses including having the largest bakery in her town before she left everything to save her life when there was a political regime that threatened her life.

As a teenager I started working in retail stores and immediately began to notice systems (or the lack of them) and noticing what worked and didn't. By the time I was 19, I was doing secretarial work in a large publishing company in the heart of Hollywood. Some of the Masters I learned the most from were women who ran the offices of attorneys and executives. They ran their lives – the same way I later ran the lives of some of my partners – through systems that supported them in bringing their gifts to the world!

For eight years I worked in the legal system both in Los Angeles and Hawaii. First as an assistant legal secretary, later as a Spanish and English interpreter, and finally as an official court reporter.

After my first administrative job – while I went to college – with *Petersen Publishing* that published *Surfing Magazine* (incidentally, down the street from Hugh Hefner's offices that housed *Playboy Magazine*), I was a part-time assistant legal secretary in Louie Edelberg's legal offices on Wilshire Boulevard where I met my first organizational Master.

Unfortunately, I didn't have enough distinctions about organizational systems to know how brilliant she was until many years later when I had only met a few master like her! I wish I could remember her name, find her and share with her the contribution she made to my life and to so many other entrepreneurs.

She would have loved seeing how far her systems have gone – there are very successful business owners in the heart of Shanghai, Beijing, Kuala Lumpur, Singapore, India, and other exotic, far away lands that are utilizing her systems to create wealth!

She is the one that taught me what I ended up calling the *Personal Productivity System,* which guides you to set up a totally efficient desk and office that when followed exactly, support off-the-charts productivity. It has been applied, tested and improved by entrepreneurs, administrative assistants, and others. You can find it in Chapter 2 of the *Money-Making Systems* manual. It even has a ready-made shopping list that you can take to any office supply store or buy online and set up the system!

As I started working as a professional interpreter, the cases took me to law firms, doctors and other professionals' offices and organizations where I continued to distinguish *good* systems from *poor* ones. I was curious as to why there was such a difference so I started looking for the distinctions. I could see that there were some offices that ran smoothly – and it was definitely clear when offices were not so blessed (desks and offices that looked like a bomb had hit them).

I gathered powerful distinctions (and tremendous knowledge) as I worked with attorneys. Some thought of court reporters as a piece of furniture and said many things that probably should have never have been said outside of their circle of colleagues and staff. To this day, I still use some of the strategies and negotiating skills that I learned from some of the best – and what to believe or not!

As an interpreter and court reporter on a daily basis, I was privy to discussions, trials, hearings and depositions which covered civil and criminal cases. I learned tremendously about business and people!

I saw people constantly fighting and attempting to make others responsible for their mistakes, misfortunes, and grief. Watching that behavior day after day got me to start thinking about how we humans behave and react to stressful situations – the subject is so large that it's going to require a whole other book!

The questioning in my mind that started in the legal environment later supported me to understand the many *Personal Development* tools and principles that I ended up using in building the various businesses that I have owned.

Early in the process of attending the first *Burklyn Business School for Entrepreneurs,* I found my passion and purpose. I was part of the team that pioneered the business of **transformational, experiential, entrepreneurial education.** We were the first... this passion and purpose continues for me to this day.

I have had some magnificent Masters through the decades of doing my work. In this book series I will share some of the wisdom and the many lessons learned from them. I am forever grateful for their contribution to my well-being and to whom I have become...

The Power of Duplication for Better Leverage:

I could see that one of the keys to successful systems was duplication that could easily be understood and repeated by almost anyone. In other words, new employees or a temporary staff member (or volunteer) could step right in and successfully perform almost any job in a very short time because the tasks to be performed were so clearly defined and documented.

When I was hired to work as a Certified Shorthand Reporter (CSR) in one of the most comprehensive and complex (yet organized) systems in the world – the Los Angeles Municipal Court System, I saw a sample of a smooth-running system that I am sure many wished it hadn't been so – many criminals would have loved to have had their records lost! That was an example of a comprehensive system at work that kept track of every piece of paper and information related to the case in a file. It was extraordinary.

My job was in the Criminal Courts building. The building was made famous by the O.J. Simpson trial. It has 19 floors of courts, offices and temporary lock-ups. What struck me most was that even with the thousands of cases moving through the courts every week, any bit of information on any case could be located from the file folders kept on said case.

This was before computers kept track of records. The case files had specific steps for tracking and for updating any case-related notes. That system was absolutely amazing. This is where the saying "he has a file a foot tall" comes from. They were actual physical files.

This was a crucial lesson for me because it demonstrated that even in a huge organization with a well thought-out and well-executed system, it is possible to keep track of a single piece of paper.

Once I understood this, I saw that any office or organization could be organized. I've always loved it when things were organized. I knew that I had to learn how to consistently keep my paperwork and documents in order – and have those around me do the same.

You could say it was my passion to discover how to master the details of a job or process and then pass that knowledge along to other people. It is no wonder that I ended up organizing and running business school programs for entrepreneurs! Some highly-driven entrepreneurs do not have the tendency to be orderly nor organized and need to have support staff to keep them on track.

Do you want to have a business or organization that runs and functions as an organized system, complete with happy, productive people? I suggest that you use our organizational manual *Money-Making Systems*. It can serve as a virtual mentor for learning how to be organized and create mega-efficient offices physically and through team-building.

The principles I am passing along are the result of many years of mistakes, trials, and successes by many people. Please allow me to be a messenger to you... to pass to you these tools created by Masters and hopefully save you years of hard work, pain, struggle, and money!

Once your systems are defined, documented and in place, there are some very important keys to becoming a Master in your field:

Key principle #1: Learn From Other People's Mistakes and Experiences.

Have you ever noticed that your best lessons are learned from mistakes? You can also learn from other people's mistakes and experiences!

This is the value of working with an experienced Master. They help us identify our mistakes and can recommend what needs to be done to correct as quickly as possible. The key is to be humble enough to learn from them...

Some Tips From My Experience —

From going in and out of many different offices in my legal career, I soon identified that there were three types of dysfunctional office "systems":

- Offices that looked like a bomb hit them so no one could find anything without tearing the place apart.

- Some offices that looked impeccable with everything in its place but you didn't know where to start or what to do if something needed to be located. A pretty maze with no map to guide you to the treasure!

- Then there were the offices where there were files and piles of papers everywhere. At first glance, it looked hopeless and yet I could tell there was a "system" of organization because I could ask *the* key person for a particular piece of paper and they could always find it! Perhaps "system" is not the right term here. Perhaps the right term would be that it is a *personal* "filing system" that is in the mind of just *one* person. The challenge with this type of "system" is that only that one person could find the documents needed – no easy-to-use system in place!

The biggest problem with a "system" of this type was that if anything went wrong, or *the* person was out of the office and someone else needed a file, it could not be found.

What offices like these lacked was LEVERAGE. A subject that will be discussed in detail shortly.

Who is Really in Charge?

In each office that I worked in, I learned that it was important to find out who was the "power behind the power." I then made that person my "mentor" (though I didn't use that term then) and found ways to support her (they were all women then) in making it easier for them to do their job. I did this instinctively in the process of learning how to improve the administrative tasks that I was starting to master myself.

Finding the "power behind the power" is crucial if you are in sales. Trust me… if you want to sell something to a company you need to determine who is the real decision-maker to sell your product or service to. Most offices are run by someone who many times sits in a back room running the business – most likely a quiet person who may not be very visible or getting much credit in public.

Find out who the "real boss" is in a business you are interested in doing business with and give them what they need to make their job easier, more efficiently in less time and bring in more profits. You have a much better chance of not only making a sale… you may now have a new ally who may give you referrals!

Masters in organizations usually have – and can show you – their highly duplicatable systems. You just have to know whom and how to ask.

It is important to realize that Masters are everywhere and the more you pay attention to both the good and the bad elements of other people's systems, you will reap the rewards. Your best teachers show up where people are making mistakes as well as where all their systems are humming. This is because you can often learn as much from observing what NOT to do along with looking for the best practices. Write down your insights for future reference and training and start putting your insights to work.

Key principle #2: Make It Safe and Profitable for Team Members to Teach Others Their Job.

I spent some time as a temporary (temp) worker. This experience allowed me to look at different office systems, and it was a great learning experience. On one of my assignments, I worked in the filing department of a large insurance company. Their filing system was so difficult and so complicated that there was no easy way to step into it.

It appeared as if someone had thought that if they could make it incredibly complicated no one else would be able to figure it out and would give them better job security. This was not at all necessary, of course, and it certainly made it hard for a temp like me to quickly take on the tasks of that job. I wanted to do a good job, but it was next to impossible because I didn't have a manual or clear systems of what I was supposed to do. This was a poorly managed operation!

16

Brightness of the Future:

"Brightness of the future" means that there is an opportunity for growth and advancement in a company or organization. A business that hasn't established "brightness of the future" in its policies and practices for key people (especially behind the scenes), they will not be inspired to duplicate themselves. They will keep their best systems and practices a secret.

If they don't believe that they will have a better job to move to if they lose the one that they have, it's almost a survival mechanism. They will be reluctant to document their positions and to put everything they do in writing in manuals or guidelines for others to follow. They could subconsciously be consumed by the fear that someone else might come in and take over their job.

When that type of thinking is rampant in a company, the talented people have no reason to be faithful nor to stay for a long time – eventually, they do leave for a variety of reasons and businesses can quickly go into a crisis. It can take weeks, even months, to re-create any system that was dependent on the skills of a person who is no longer available.

Document Jobs So Anyone Can Do Them:

Ideally, if a company's systems are well documented in manuals, job descriptions, or guidelines, then ANY qualified person for that job can step in and duplicate the position, and their chances of staying on track are highly magnified. You are now covered when employees move up or out. This is another way of leveraging yourself.

Begin the manuals (and job descriptions, if needed) with a statement as to why and how it is a benefit for the company – and everyone in it – to document and manualize the elements of their jobs so that others can easily do the tasks. Then people are willing to teach their techniques and systems to others because a path of advancement is attached to the policy of writing up job descriptions and distinctions of that job.

Many companies do regular cross-training. It gives everyone a chance to learn about all the aspects of what makes the business "tick" and it also protects the business from being left in the lurch should someone suddenly not show up for work.

This principle of duplication through documentation is so important! We've devoted a whole chapter in our *Money-Making Systems* manual which I wrote from my experiences in the legal systems that I have been describing: http://www.MoneyandYou.com/money-making-systems/

Basically, each person should be responsible and encouraged to keep updating a complete job description on their position, and someone should be responsible to continually add it to a company *Operations Manual*. It should include the details on how to do all the specific tasks required by that job each day, weekly, monthly or periodically. If you are the business owner, it's up to you to give those directives.

If you are an employee and share this distinction with the business owner that you work for, it will favorably increase their experience of you and possibly see you in a more positive light that could lead you to promotions or a management position if you are not there yet.

If you make it attractive and mandatory for people to teach others how to do their job, people will be motivated to expand their skills, make improvements, and move upwards in the organization. The spirit of teamwork will increase as people cross-train others on their jobs. Stress and tension will decrease because others can jump in to help when deadlines need to be met. You will love the synergy that this distinction will generate in your organization!

A Business Is A Living Organism:

When the systems that I have recommended are in place, each person becomes a mentor to another person. The business expands and grows, and people feel that they matter and are making a positive contribution to the bottom line of the company's – this raises their self-esteem.

You will find out how important that is as I continue to share what it takes to have a systems-based organization in today's rapidly changing world – and because a business is a living organism.

Systems must be continually improved and be able to easily flow with changes if you want a business to grow and be prosperous. The only thing that is certain is change both with the people in it and the economy it lives in. This is a fact you can count on.

Because each person is a unique human being, the need for systems that work is paramount. If you set up systems that are easy to follow, reliable and predictable then regardless of who is in which job or who is running it, the organization will function smoothly.

Set it up so that someone is constantly revising and updating your systems as everyone learns what makes your offices and business more efficient; on-going cross-training and documentation is important all the time. Teach your people to tell each other when they have learned from a mistake. Let each person be a mentor to their co-workers and reward them every time a mistake gets prevented from ever happening again.

A Master – Dr. R. Buckminster Fuller:

Through our live training programs, podcasts, Google Hangouts, Webinars, books, blogs and Social Media, we introduce amazing business, organizational and new-thought Masters such as Buckminster Fuller ("Bucky"). We had the privilege of having him teach at our original *Burklyn Business School* (which evolved to the *Excellerated Business School® for Entrepreneurs)* six years in a row from 1978 until just before his passing on July 1, 1983. We also had the opportunity to host his longest live event for six days entitled *The Future of Business* where he taught some of his most profound teachings to over 100 entrepreneurs and business owners.

One of his most important teachings was:

"The greatest mistake human beings make is to make themselves wrong for making mistakes. It is our natural way of learning..."

Bucky is known by many as the "the planet's friendly genius," and perhaps one of the best-known American thinkers of the 20th century. He was an architect, mathematician, author, designer, cosmetologist, scientist, inventor, and philosopher. He coined the words: "synergy" and "Spaceship Earth." He developed the *World Game*; invented his own mathematics known a Synergetics; created the geodesic dome, and was recognized throughout the world for his creative contributions to technology and the future. It has been predicted that in the 21st century, he will be placed alongside Einstein, Copernicus and Newton for his tremendous contribution to the well-being of humanity and our world. He was an avid environmentalist as far back as the 1930's.

Bucky is missed by all who knew him. Many keep learning about him and his work through our programs, and through the work done by some of our graduates like Peter Meisen who has the www.GENI.org organization.

Also from Randolph Craft who has created a library of videos of the live program where Bucky shared his teachings for six days.

All of our work continues to educate many globally about Bucky's generalized principles and steps that need to be taken in order to survive as a species. Some are recommended in Bucky's book, *Critical Path*. You can find many of his books at http://www.BFI.org

Through our work, training materials and our graduates' work, Bucky's legacy will live on. Use this link to see the many organizations dedicated to his work: http://www.moneyandyou.com/buckminster-fuller/

You read earlier on the question that we live by that was inspired by Bucky. If you wish to download some great photos that I have taken around the world (including Antarctica) with Bucky's empowering question go to my http://www.Facebook.com/DCCordovaFriends and pass the good word!

Chapter 1 – Review

Key Principle #1

Learn from other people's mistakes.

Key Principle #2

Make it attractive for people to teach others.

1. **A Master is important to a successful business career because:**

    A. They have achieved mastery in their endeavor.

    B. They teach "tricks of the trade." shortening the learning curve.

    C. We can learn from their mistakes.

2. **All successful business systems can be duplicated** and understood by anyone.

3. **Good office communications systems are a must.** SYSTEMS CAN BE SIMPLE.

4. **"No brightness of the future"** causes people to hang on to their jobs for fear that nothing else is out there.

5. **Document everything** so anyone can do it, and more are cross trained.

Chapter 2

Niche – Finding Your Passion

If you want to be highly successful, find a niche.

What is a niche? It's a product or service that no one (or a few) is offering in the marketplace. It is usually in a specialized area that meets a want or fills the need of an identifiable group of people.

I know this sounds a little old, and it's such a great example of a specialized niche: the *Personal Computer*, fondly known to its users as the *"PC."* Before the PC entered our lives, all there was were *mainframes* – large, room-sized computers that dominated the computing world; and *mini-computers* – the kind that would not fit on a desk and took specialists to run and operate. While the existence of computers was common knowledge, they were never considered as useful to the general consumer. An entirely new niche was born when a couple of whiz kids – working their way through college by tinkering with electronics – developed something in their garage that they thought would be useful.

At the time, the only small computers on the market required assembly and came as a *kit*. These primitive boxes were operated by manipulating levers, dial, and lights. This kit computer was of interest only to hard-core computer scientists and hobbyists. Steve Jobs and Steve Wozniac, two enterprising young men living in what is now known as the Silicon Valley area of Northern California, saw a need that wasn't being filled. Fascinated with what they could make these little kits, they created a case to hold the inner workings, gave the operator an easy-to-use keyboard for the input and, voila! The first "user-friendly" PC was born... It was a personal computer that anyone could operate!

There are several stories of why they called their product and their company *Apple Computer*. One, Jobs and Wozniak wanted their start-up to be in front of *Atari* in the phone book. Another, they wanted to distance themselves from the cold, complicated imagery created by other computer companies like *IBM* and *Digital Equipment*. Lastly, they wanted to honor *Apple Records*, the music label of the *Beatles* – later they were sued for that name, but it got resolved.

Eventually, the name was changed to just *Apple* when they started expanding their product line. Branding is so important... and there are many wonderful Masters out there that can guide you through that intricate field.

The young men's invention revolutionized the way the world would operate from that point forward because it gave the general population easier access to real computer power and they created a consumer-based product people would want to buy for themselves.

The *Apple* computer wasn't the first computer. But it met a need not met by any other product or manufacturer. In other words, it was an important variation in an existing market (computers), and it fitted perfectly into a space (a niche) that wasn't being filled by the two corporate computer giants at the time — *IBM* and *Hewlett-Packard*. Not only did it bring computing power to the masses, thus creating a whole new marketplace, but it revolutionized the one that already existed!

Apple had found a need and filled it. The rest is history. And in case you don't know their current stats: *Apple* is the world's largest information technology company by revenue, the world's largest technology company by total assets, and the world's second-largest mobile phone manufacturer. On November 25, 2014, in addition to being the largest publicly traded corporation in the world by market capitalization, Apple became the first U.S. company to be valued at over US$700 billion. The company employs 115,000 permanent full-time employees as of July 2015 and maintains 453 retail stores in 16 countries as of March 2015.

Look around you for gaps in society that you can fill with a product or service! The more niches you identify, the closer you are to finding your path to passion and purpose like I have!

A Successful Franchise Model — McDonald's:

Another great old example of a "niche-creating" company is McDonald's. At the time it started, there were many restaurants, coffee shops, and drive-in fast-food restaurants in the USA, plus others had come up with the idea of selling a "ready-made" hamburger at a very low price from several different similar facilities. But McDonald's set out to carve a niche for itself.

Everyone knows that McDonald's doesn't necessarily make the best hamburgers (and more) in the world. But what you can count is that you can expect the same, predictable size, shape and quality of a hamburger, french fries, and now a much more varied menu every time you eat there anywhere in the world – same for the type of decor, uniforms and architecture at many McDonald's around the world.

What made McDonald's famous was the system that all McDonald's franchise owners could duplicate. In other words, McDonald's was not as much in the hamburger business as in the business of selling you the real estate and the "system" for making and selling hamburgers!

Ray Kroc, the owner, was an outstanding businessman who was brilliant at marketing. Kroc knew that customers like to know what to expect. He knew that people want predictability. They thrive on security. They are most happy when they can count on finding what they expect when they are in a hurry.

What gives McDonald's its predictability are the SYSTEMS that are in place for every aspect of the business.

Now if you are thinking, *"Why should I learn about how a franchise works? I'm never going to own a franchise,"* as your mentor at this moment, I invite you to apply the principles being taught in this book and allow yourself to let go of pre-conceived beliefs and limited attitudes.

My best advice (based on decades of experience) is that whether or not you ever plan to franchise or duplicate your business, highly effective and functioning systems should be in place as if you were.

These systems make it possible for anyone to operate your business so you won't always have to be there... Freedom!

By the way, I highly recommend you read anything you can about Ray Kroc. It's a mature company, and there is much to be learned. He believed in and practiced many of the business principles we teach. He differed from us in philosophy in one area that we feel quite strongly about... that of making *mistakes*.

Kroc was a perfectionist, and he believed that people should be trained so well that they would "never make a mistake." We tell you to give yourself permission TO make mistakes. While it might be ideal if there were no mistakes, we believe that mistakes actually make you stronger. When you hold mistakes as "learning experiences," you can form a firm foundation of creativity on which to build.

Something must have worked! McDonald's is the world's largest chain of hamburger fast food restaurants, serving around 68 million customers daily in 119 countries across more than 36,000 outlets!

John Wooden, the head coach for the winningest UCLA basketball team ever (over 11 years without a loss) was asked why his team won so many games. His reply was, "we make more mistakes than any other team."

In other words, when you have a "go for it" attitude and allow yourself to make mistakes, you quickly discover through personal experience what works and what doesn't work. And if something doesn't work... adjust and take more action. If something does work... refine it and put it into your systems!

Niches Are Everywhere:

If you look around at businesses, you'll see many successful companies that have found a niche for themselves. Note what they do and learn from that.

You can be successful by emulating a successful niche – not an exact copy but improving it, making it better, cheaper or more efficient. The real key to reaching high levels of profitability is identifying a need and filling it with better components, attributes, or benefits!

In this book, we don't promote or invalidate any specific type of business as there are many ways to build successful organizations. The key to success is learning how to find a niche of your own and then applying the principles and tools I share here with you. When you apply these tools and approaches, you will have the groundwork to build your own successful organization and have a head start on creating that "brightness of future" for you and your team!

Do Something Good For Others:

One of the things we can predict from our experience is that the most successful businesses in the 21st century will be the ones that in some way contribute to society. Choose to make things a little better for all concerned and endeavor to "do no harm" to people or the environment. If every company followed this recommendation, our world would be a better place. In addition, many people would actually discover a novel way of doing business!

Don't overlook the many new niches that exist (or are waiting to be discovered) because of the environmental issues in our world today and solving other 21st century challenges. There are opportunities waiting everywhere for you to create a successful business solving a problem.

If you live in an area or a country that is not a "trendsetter," or in an environment that doesn't encourage or promote innovation, you may have to travel to other parts of the world that are the forerunners of certain industries that pique your interest. You can take those niche ideas back to your homeland and have a highly successful business. Having an open mind and looking actively for new paradigms is a key to finding money-making niches.

The Hour Glass — An Asia Business Success Story:

Another organization we like to mention is *The Hour Glass*, the leading specialist watch retailer created and shaped by our friend and mentor, Jannie Chan (formerly Tay). *The Hour Glass* was developed from a one-store operation in 1979 to a noted brand with an extensive network of boutiques located in prime shopping districts across Asia-Pacific region. Today, this publicly held company's portfolio also includes a range of interests focused largely on high-end commercial and retail properties.

Jannie, together with her team, opened a niche in Asia for anyone to wear luxury watches as jewelry pieces and in doing so became a major trendsetter. She embraces and uses the technology shared in this book. One of her greatest gifts to us is her constant reminder that principles don't mean anything unless applied to real life and business experience. Your practice of the principles and experience in applying them is what develops wisdom, and then success follows. Jannie Chan's life and success story is known by many in Asia and has been shared in her own book, *Time to Live*.

How To Develop Your Niche:

1. Handle Survival

It is not easy to be creative when you have bill collectors at the door. In order for you to develop a successful business or organization, you have to develop good money habits.

As a rule of thumb, you should have enough money set aside to be able to pay for the basics: mortgage or rent, basic bills, food, auto expenses, insurance, etc. for at least 6 months. This will reduce stress if your business is just getting launched or going through a downturn or you are re-adjusting to a market shift.

Whether you are using your savings, nest egg, getting support from your family or using a loan from the bank, your chances for success may be in direct proportion to your ability to handle your finances.

Statistics from governments around the world indicate that most new businesses fail. My sense is that a large number of these failed businesses are a result of the fact that so many people do not take the time to plan and educate themselves on the fundamentals of how a business is successfully built; how money works – having financial literacy. That's important whether you are a business owner or part of an entrepreneurial team or an employee.

2. Have A Plan Of Action

Your plan is the key to your success. What kind of plan? Any written plan will do as long as you make one and follow it.

The word "plan" has been overused, and it seems to have lost its meaning. I thought it would be interesting to consult my dictionary and thesaurus to get more of the "flavor" of the word to give you another point of view from which to consider this topic.

The word PLAN is defined in the dictionary as both a noun and a verb. Let's look first at the noun form for some clarity on what a PLAN really is. You can consider your plan to be a conception, design, scheme, strategy, method, order, pattern, system, blueprint, diagram, sketch, ambition, intention or purpose.

Looking at PLAN as a verb gives you an action to take. Consider that PLAN could be an *intention to arrange, design, devise, map out, chart, organize, outline, prepare aim, intend, or propose a direction* for your business.

In other publications, we'll teach you a simple form of planning that we teach at our *Excellerated Business Schools® for Entrepreneurs* by Randolph Craft called PERT (Program Evaluation Review Technique). We learned that technique from the original creator, Jim Halcomb, who designed the PERT chart for NASA that took man to the moon ahead of schedule.

Bottom line, have a written plan of action, then follow it – even if it is only a piece of paper stuck on your refrigerator – just kidding! I'd recommend that you do some research on the best planning software in the market – or reach out to Randolph Craft. His contact is in the *More Information and Resources* area in the back of this book.

3. Ask Yourself: What would you do if you had all the money in the world?

This question should be considered more from the metaphysical standpoint than technically, as this question offers a very important perspective for looking at your business. If money is no longer a concern, you can do whatever you love – whatever makes your heart sing!

Are you doing what you love? That thing that you love to do is one of your "gifts." But because it is so easy for you to do, many people overlook it and think it is "no big deal"! This is understandable because our gifts and talents are uniquely expressed in and through us. We often perform our business in our own special way which also creates a special niche.

This suggestion comes from our many years in the field of entrepreneurial education. We've discovered that once a person becomes clear on what they love to do the most, they can turn that love into a business! This is one of the secrets of success… do what you LOVE!

Masters who are working on their succession plans notice those who are really "turned on" by what they are doing. Work is no longer work… it's play. They look for the ones who love their work so much they seem to get lost in time and seldom consider whether it is time to quit work or not. They know they have found the right person when they have to remind them to go home!

4. Do your market and financial research

Traditional business schools used to teach people to create a need – and "old-fashioned," out-of-step business people are still promoting that old thinking. One of our instructors at our business school in 1978, Dr. Bucky Fuller, taught us to just look around and see what is needed and wanted… and create a business around that need (niche) – and ideally, one that adds value to humanity.

Today enterprising entrepreneurs are doing this more and more. This is what the founders of *Apple* did. They found a need and filled it.

If you wish to revamp your business to be more up to date with today's business trends, do your market research and take a look at the technologies available that you can use to improve your business.

If you are just starting out, look at the top five industries that are going to thrive in the future and choose one that fits your temperament, personality style, and your heart's desires. Then do the financial research around that industry and choose clearly which direction you wish to take.

Research Research Research... Google makes it so easy... and this will also support you in continuing to answer:

How Do You Find A Need?

To discover what people want, do market research. First, ask yourself: what is missing in the areas that are of interest to you? Ask others what they notice is missing for them or what they wish they could have or do.

There are many things that people need and want and would be willing to pay for that don't currently exist in the marketplace. If you can't find it for sale anywhere, this is a sign. You can even ask them how much they would be willing to pay for those products or services if they became available.

When considering developing your ideal niche some important questions to ask:

- Does your niche exist? (If it's commonly done, then it isn't a niche)
- Who says it is needed? (And would they buy it from you if you had it?)
- Where do the people that need it "hang out"? (So you can let them know when you have it)
- Is there already something similar to the niche you want to develop that already exists? If so, how is it being done? Can you improve on it?

- Is there a person or organization that could teach you something more about what you want to develop?
- If your niche idea doesn't already exist, what do you need to do to start developing it?

And be open to coming up with more questions – have a mastermind group support you. Join groups that are like-minded and keep researching!

Be FIRST... or Be the BEST:

You don't always have to be first with a niche to be famous or successful... but it helps.

We all know that Charles Lindberg was the first man to fly solo across the Atlantic and that Amelia Earhart was the first woman... but who were the second man and woman?

If you can't be first, then you need to be the best... or the best known.

How would you do this? What could you do differently to get the attention, the press, a Social Media buzz, a great reputation? This inquiry becomes a great game and one that is fun to play when you are looking at doing what you love.

Develop your niche around the answers to these questions:

Can you be the first in your niche?

Would your current level of fame be enough to give you a significant edge? (This is why companies pay celebrities to endorse their products).

Could you advertise or popularize your product or service significantly better than your competition?

The answers will point to how you should position yourself and where to focus your promotional endeavors and advertising.

Use the answers to discover how to communicate your features and benefits. They will tell you to whom to direct your advertising (your target) and where to advertise to reach them (target marketplace).

Before The Cash Register Rings:

Before getting started, you should consider the answers to these important financial questions:

- How much money do I need to live for the next six months?

- How much capital do I need to begin this business?

- Who or what are my sources for that money? Banks? Grants? Small Business Administration (SBA) in the USA? Other government institutions in other countries? Family? Savings? Investors? Friends?

- What do I need to know to set up a business in this niche? Are there licensing requirements? Any special training required? What are the legal considerations? What are the space and site regulations?

- Have I set my plan up around the questions in the *Blueprint for Success* (Available as a bonus in http://www.MoneyandYou.com/Book)

The bottom line when it comes to making money in a business and being successful is relatively simple:

- Find out what people want
- Deliver it better than anyone else
- Be consistent with your values
- Do what you love
- Set up an "Economic Engine" to create profits
- Put systems in place – plan on selling in 5 years – whether you do or not – it's irrelevant – it's about the systems
- Take action!

5. "The Law of Non-Attachment" – Be willing to not have it!

There is another valuable metaphysical principle to understand and apply: "The Law of Non-Attachment." In other words, if there's something that we want so much, we must be willing to let it go. Release all attachment to it and be willing NOT to have it. When we let something go, it can freely flow. Let it go and if it is yours and right for you, it will return to you.

Another way of saying this – if you are attached to a particular outcome, you will manipulate situations and others to get what you are trying to achieve. If you are not attached, you will set your goal(s), take the right steps to make it happen and then let go and allow for the outcome. Save your energy... I know for those that love to control situations, this is counter-intuitive – and test it next time you set your sights on a particular outcome.

This will also make more sense when you find your niche and begin developing your business. Ask others who have already found their niche: "was there a time when you had to be willing to give it up before you could really have it"?

We often think we know the best way to express our real talents. The fact is that there are unlimited opportunities. If we are stuck on doing something a particular way, it may not be in our best interest in the long run.

When we stop insisting that things be a certain way, we often find that there is something even better waiting for us that we couldn't see until we let go. In future writings, I'll be covering the generalized principle of *Precession*, the scientific explanation of ripple effects. In short, when one takes action, results – both expected and unexpected – will occur. More to come on *Precession*!

Personal Integrity:

Sometimes when people are driven by ego only, they often do things that are out of integrity... both with themselves and society. While the business might succeed for a while – making them lots of money – in the long run compromising their integrity will keep them from being successful in all areas of their lives – not to mention being at peace with themselves.

No amount of money can make up for the lack of peace we feel when we are out of alignment with our hearts. The key is whether we are holding onto something (or a point of view) out of fear. Perhaps that we may not have... or be enough.

The laws of the Universe function perfectly every time and we always get what we really expect, whether it's scarcity, sufficiency or abundance. Henry Ford brought this point home in regard to the abundance of capability within each of us with his famous quote, *"Whether you think you can or you think you can't, you're right"*!

6. Clearly choose it!

Clearly choosing every aspect of your business is probably the most important point we can make on the subject of niche because you will be doing it for a long time if you are successful – so you might as well choose a business that involves something you LOVE to do.

Choosing means *to take full responsibility for it and after all the considerations around the subject.* If you have clearly chosen it, focus on it and stay with it until the business succeeds. Set your standards of measurement up front. This conscious decision and commitment to your choice will provide a sense of freedom that, in turn, will give you a great sense of purpose.

One of the reasons you have to clearly choose it is because you'll be spending a lot of time in the business. If it isn't your real choice, you'll probably give up at some point. Growing successful businesses takes time!

Lag Time + Consistent Effort = Success

Some people mistakenly think that when they go into business for themselves, they will know whether it is going to be successful or not within the first six months to a year. This would be nice, but we find that it usually takes from two to five years for a business to be consistently profitable. Successful business people understand this and adjust their expectations in line with this fact.

Business is like anything you grow. It has to go through a gestation period before it matures. The business term that describes this natural law of gestation is called "LAG." In this instance, it means that it could take years of hard work before you see the fruits of your labor.

We can illustrate the principle of lag best with the analogy of growing a fruit tree...

First, you have to make a plan. You can only choose which type of fruit tree to plant after you decide what outcome you really want – fruit for canning, fruit for eating off the tree, fruit for selling at the market – after you can plan the location of the tree, based on all your options. All of this is part of your **market research** including the type and size of the tree that will fit in your chosen location.

Second, you have to carefully prepare the soil. As part of your market and financial research, you need to find out what it would take to maintain the best environment for the tree. Once you know that you have the right soil and climate and have planted the seed, you'll have to know the right amount of water and light to give it – based on the type of tree it is.

Third, you plant the seed, cover it with dirt and trust what you can't see. In the face of no immediate evidence, you have to be willing to wait for it (not have it.)

Fourth, you have to clearly choose it and take personal responsibility for it. You make sure it gets water and fertilizer regularly – merely on the faith that it will grow.

For a quite a while there will be no indication on the surface that it is going to be a healthy (successful) tree, because it is establishing a strong foundation of roots. Most plants grow down before they grow upwards where you can see and measure their progress.

Fifth, you help the tree trunk to grow straight and strong by tying it loosely to a stake while it is in its early growth period. You know the tree needs to sacrifice a little *comfort* initially in order to grow straight and tall.

And finally, when it begins to produce fruit, you only get the real harvest from the tree after it has been an established tree for a couple of years. This is considered LAG time.

You can now see your success in every inch of growth the tree makes. You know it was a right idea by the joy you feel when you look at it, even when you spend time removing the weeds and weaker seedlings (which allows it more room to develop even stronger roots).

Do you have the patience to keep going and growing through the lag time? Take a look and see if you have the persistence and stamina to go into a business that may take two to five years (or more) to develop before you begin to see a decent profit. That is the commitment that it will most likely take in order to see the "fruits" of your labor!

This is also a good thought-process if you are considering going into a partnership with someone – are you willing to stay with that person or group a long time before enjoying the fruits of your labor?

Once you have clearly chosen all the pertinent aspects of your business, congratulations! You can now start to put the principles of **Leverage** to work and begin to duplicate yourself and your systems so you can replace yourself and work ON your business and not IN it.

Some questions you might find helpful to ask in identifying your "passion" or purpose in life:

- If you could do anything you wanted to do and had no money concerns, what would you choose to do?

- What do you do that seems "simple" to you but other people constantly acknowledge you for it?

- What do other people say your unique personal qualities are? Humor? Enthusiasm? Creativity?

- What three or four words describe the things you like to do? Support? Inspire? Execute? Lead?

- What is your ideal working environment and what activities would you like to be doing? Working with your hands? Working with people? Working with numbers? Solving challenges? Analyzing things?

- What types of clothes would you ideally be able to wear to go to work in? Casual? Dressy? Expensive? Inexpensive? High fashion? Trendy?

- What type of clothes would the others who interact with you be wearing?

- What kinds of conversations would you be having? Negotiating? Brainstorming? Giving instructions? Creating new ideas?

- Where would you be doing your work? In your home? At a computer? On the phone? In others' offices? In a tall office building? At the beach? On the road in your car? On a cruise ship? At Starbucks?

- What would you do if you knew you couldn't fail?

- What would the world be like if you (and everyone else) were working in their ideal niche, doing what they loved?

- What would excite you so much that you could hardly get to sleep at night – and you could hardly wait to get up in the morning – so you could go to work? Do?

In our *Money & You* program, we have a flipchart with the statement: *Clarity Lead to Power...* Answer those questions and it will greatly increase your clarity!

May The Niche Be With You...!

Chapter 2 – Review

Niche: a specialized area that meets a "want" or fills a "need" of an identifiable group of people.

1. **How to develop a Niche:**

   a. **Handle survival** – success may be in direct proportion to your ability to handle your finances.

   b. **Have a plan of action** – bottom line, have a written plan of action, then follow it.

   c. **Ask yourself;** what would I do if I had all the money in the world? One of the secrets of success… do what you LOVE!

   d. **Do your market and financial research** – look at the top five industries that are going to thrive in the future and choose one that fits your temperament, personality, style, and your heart's desires.

   e. **Be willing to not have it** – when we let something go, we can freely have it.

   f. **Clearly choose it** – take full responsibility for it and stay with it until the business succeeds.

2. **Make your plan well documented** as if you will be franchising.

3. **Have a "go for it" attitude** and allow for mistakes. Discovery comes from what does as well as what doesn't work.

4. **Lag Time + Consistent Effort = Success.** It usually takes two to five years for a business to be consistently profitable.

5.   **Key qualities** for succeeding in a niche business that you have been introduced to while reading this book are:

        i.   Patience
        ii.   Persistence
        iii.   Responsibility
        iv.   Joy
        v.   Integrity
        vi.   Commitment

Chapter 3

Leverage

The Number 1 Key to Creating Profits for YOU and Your Organization – Leverage! This is a term that is now commonly known, but when I joined the *Burklyn* organization that was first pioneering the transformational, experiential, entrepreneurial industry, it was only used in finance, real estate, stocks, and bonds – in Wall Street. It was not used in the entrepreneurial context that it is used today.

A good sample of *leverage* is when you purchase a costly asset and you only pay a small percentage of the total cost and the balance of the funds necessary to complete the transaction is financed by a bank or lender, i.e. when purchasing a home. In the US it's called a "down payment" which could be 10% or 20% of the total cost – in other countries, it could be much higher.

A physical illustration of *leverage* would be a children's teeter-totter in a playground. It consists of a plank sitting on a bar, and it only needs the weight of a child to lift another child on the other end of the plank. An example is in construction before they had the machinery to lift heavy objects. They would use a plank on a pivot point or a rock, and they would use the long end to lift a heavy load on the other end.

Over the years, we have expanded the definition of *leverage* – besides leveraging money, we can *leverage* ourselves through systems, people, networks – and one can even *leverage* knowledge, contacts! *Leverage* can be used in many different ways – it's a matter of truly understanding the principle.

Most small business owners, managers (and most of the general population) works much harder than necessary because they don't understand *leverage!*

Some people think they do... but if right now you are not able to leave your business and have it fully functioning without you through systems, then you don't really understand or know how to apply *leverage* into your business.

If right now you can't afford to fly anywhere in the world first (or business) class, go to a five-star resort, stay in any room that you wish, enjoy the spa services or eat in any restaurant of your choice – while there is "automatic" or multiple sources of income going into your bank account – then you don't understand *leverage!*

You truly know *leverage* if your results show that you do!

In our *Money & You*® program we spend hours playing certain games and exercises to support the participants to realize whether they really understand *leverage...* We have a saying:

If you don't understand leverage, you work too hard!

Most business people know that one can leverage money and products. One more key distinction to this principle: *leverage* YOURSELF through PEOPLE, networks, affiliates, and other innovative ways that technology and the Web have made it so easy to do!

Many hands make light work... You can get more done with less effort when you can get your work done with and through others. This will allow you to duplicate your business so you can have a profitable organization even when you are not there.

Most small business owners (this is what keeps the business "small") think that only *they* know how to do the important tasks of the organization and that they are *making* more money, or *saving* it, by doing as much as they can themselves.

What they don't always realize is that they could be paying others to do what needs to be done so they can spend more time focusing on **Income Generating Activities** which will bring in more profits. Always consider delegating to a competent person that can be paid less than what you can generate!

There is tremendous information available on how to *leverage* your business through effective marketing, product distribution systems and other avenues... but not precise, effective and proven people management systems for entrepreneurs that want profitable organizations that also add value to humanity. This is one of our niches! Congratulations for taking these systems, information, and distinctions on how to *leverage* your business through people!

What is the difference between leveraging through products and people?

Products are easier to *leverage*. For example, rock stars only have to create one audio or video recording and then have it available through iTunes or YouTube and other platforms to download (and in certain countries, making copies of CD's or DVD's) and earn million of whatever currency. The right products are easy to duplicate and produce – it's a matter of having, first, the vision; next, the *Excellerated Business Success Model* in place.

People, on the other hand, are not so easy to *leverage* through. They go into organizations, relationships and exist in the world as a "total package." They have feelings, thoughts, opinions, judgments and a variety of ideas on how things ought to be done – especially if they are not experienced in your field of expertise. Theory, as opposed to reality, is rampant in inexperienced minds...

Have you ever thought to yourself "business would be a lot easier if we just didn't have to deal with the people"? The solution to this problem is what this book is about – and to give you as many systems as possible so your business or organization can grow, be easily duplicated and most importantly that it can work without you.

The systems we are covering work whether you have one person or hundreds or thousands working for you. It's a recipe – it's a model – that will allow you to create consistent results – every time – and a business that can be run efficiently.

Franchises are an excellent example of a form of *leverage* and what is possible when a business has well-defined, systematic processes.

There are many ways of leveraging your business other than franchising. But whether you think you'll ever want to franchise your business or not, we recommend you follow our suggestions and set up your business in such a way that if it were turned over to some other qualified person, it would run like clockwork... *Leverage* by creating "cookie cutter" systems!

There are also some disciplines that will keep *leverage* in your mind... Ask yourself every morning: how can I *leverage* myself, my products, my people and the resources that I have even more? How can I produce more results with even fewer resources?

"*Leverage* questions" will keep you on your toes and your mind sharp with possibilities – they will unlock the potential of your business. In many ways, these principles are like the ingredients in a recipe for a great cake. Don't substitute, don't change the ingredients or the steps if you want the same results.

This book was developed through decades of consistent study and application. It evolved from the application by many graduates of our highly successful *Money & You*® program and the *Excellerated Business School*® *for Entrepreneurs*.

The founders of the original *Burklyn Business School*, Marshall Thurber and Bobbi DePorter, along with other partners in their real estate development business grew a US$25,000 investment to US$60 million in less than 3 years using some of the same information, habits and strategies that are defined in this *Excellerated Business Success Model*.

If you apply these proven principles, your business will grow and prosper. We invite you to take notes of the different ideas and thoughts that this book is evoking. The process will help you retain and bring into your business what you are learning.

Chapter 3 – In Review

1.   **More Hands = Lighter Work**

2.   **More work is accomplished in less time** when we work with and through others.

3.   **Income Generating Activities** should be the focus of business owners, rather than focusing on work an assistant can do.

4.   **Set up your business** so that, if it were turned over to ANYONE qualified, it can run like clockwork.

5.   **Leveraging Products or Services and People is different!**

If you don't understand leverage, you work too hard!

Chapter 4

Design Your People Systems

Have you ever had the thought: "If we had better people, we wouldn't have the problems we have in our business..." This way of thinking takes the responsibility off the business owner / leader / manager and makes your people responsible and at fault for problems.

It's not always the *People* that are at fault...
It could be the *System*...

If you set up a system to support your people, your people will give you their best efforts. They will get behind your products, services, and your business 100%. Why do you think they call it *continuous improvement*?

When your people know what *100%* is supposed to be, and you have systems in place to make that a possibility, they will do their best to make your vision a reality!

What is a "system"?

There are many definitions. Webster's describes it as:

"System" - *an assemblage of things forming a connected whole; a complex but ordered whole; the body as a functioning unity; a plan or scheme; method."*

I would like to add a couple of other distinctions:

"A system with training." A system needs to be self-correcting and duplicable. It is also stable and predictable within a certain range of variation. The people within this system, when properly trained, create a very dynamic, continuously improving system.

In other words, it is not a *system* unless any properly trained person can just step in, do their job as described within the system and continuously reduce the variation toward the ideal, without constant supervision.

A Good Office Communication System:

I once saw a particularly good office communications system when I worked as a temp in a law office. Since there were over 100 attorneys plus many paralegals and other staff members moving through this organization, I was curious about how they managed to keep track of the communications amongst all those individuals.

I asked one of the secretaries, and she showed me what was called their *"Central Communications Area."* What I saw was a system that was actually very simple!

All they had was a series of "pigeon holes" or slots on a wall where all correspondence was placed for pick-up at any time. If a package was left on the ground because it was too large to fit in the individual's space, there was a note letting them know to look for it right below the slots.

It was here that I learned for the first time that **SYSTEMS CAN BE SIMPLE!** At times, they need to be set up so that a four-year-old can understand them.

The Deming System:

There are many experts who make business and OD (organization development) systems their business.

"Organization development is a system-wide application of behavioral science knowledge to the planned development and reinforcement of organizational strategies, structures, and processes for improving an organization's effectiveness."

We have always been on the lookout for Masters in their fields to learn from... One of the Masters that the creator of *Money & You,*

Marshall Thurber, found was the late American systems genius, **W. Edwards Deming**. He created a whole new paradigm called *System of Profound Knowledge.*

Deming was the one who taught the Japanese this system. Once understood, this concept changed Japan's history as well as its global reputation. Japanese products used to be described as "cheap, undependable and unreliable." Japanese-made products, especially in the electronics industry, are now known as some of the *best in the world, high quality, reliable, efficient* and *dependable.*

Initially, during World War II, Deming was employed by the U.S. Government to work on statistics and set up the systems that would make the US military more efficient.

After the war was over, his position was eliminated. His teachings were no longer considered *important.* At that time, he attempted to share his genius with American corporations in various industries, but they couldn't comprehend the importance of his work because Deming's paradigm was so far ahead of its time.

Deming began to look outside of the U.S. for those that were interested in his work and ended up offering his services to the Japanese. When they did their research on him, they recognized an opportunity to work with a genius. They took Deming up on his offer to provide them with his *System of Profound Knowledge.*

Through the application of Deming's theories, methods, and tools, the Japanese became the world-renowned Masters in productivity.

It is interesting to note that it was an American whose *Systems of Profound Knowledge* provided management methods that produced one of the most formidable competitors that Americans have to this day.

Here are two of the main theories he taught the Japanese – and which the American industry giants who had ignored him for 35 years finally got once they began to listen:

"When you have an undesirable outcome, look within the system first, you have one system and many sub-processes that are components of that single system. Then you look to the people."

"94% of failures in business outcomes are _systems_ failures."

It is human nature and easier to blame people first before ever looking at a system. However, if your rule is to look at the system first, the person who sets up the business or organization realizes that they are responsible for creating a system that works.

You study the system and get feedback from all the people using it. You keep continuously correcting as you reduce any variation leading toward the ideal.

Truth be told, too many businesses are run shabbily. Few have even mediocre standards by which to measure variation. But by introducing the philosophy of continuously improving your systems, your employees, suppliers and customers will feel the dependability of your services or products, and you'll eventually become a leader in your field.

To bring home the point, it is important to find out what your *customer* or *client* really wants and design a continuously improving system to provide that. When you do, you will have more business than you've ever imagined.

An excellent book with examples from everyday businesses that illustrate this point is *"The Flight of the Buffalo"* by Dr. James Belasco and Ralph Stayer. They suggest you:

- **Ask** "What is great performance" for your customers?"
- **Focus** on those few factors that create great performance
- **Develop** the design for each person to own and be responsible for their own great performance.
- **Align** the organization systems and structures to send a clear message as to what is necessary for great performance for both the individual and the organization.
- **Engage** the individuals – their hearts as well as their minds and hands – in the business of the business.
- **Coach** the development of individual capability and competence.
- **Learn** faster by correcting mistakes.

Here are Edwards Deming's *14 Points.* Check to see how closely your own business could be transformed through application of each of the 14 Points:

Deming's 14 Points – A Theory for Management:

1. Create constancy of purpose for improvement of product and service with the aim to become competitive, and to stay in business and to provide jobs.

2. Adopt the new philosophy by refusing to allow commonly accepted levels of delays, mistakes, defective materials and defective workmanship. Western management must awaken to the challenge and must learn their responsibilities and take on leadership for a change in their outcome!

3. Cease dependence on inspection to achieve quality. The purpose of inspection is for improvement of processes and reduction of cost.

4. End the practice of awarding business on the basis of price tag alone. Instead, minimize total cost by working with a single supplier for any one item and create a long-term relationship of loyalty and trust.

5. Improve constantly, and forever, every process for planning, production and service, and thus consistently decrease costs.

6. Institute training to make better use of all team members.

7. Adopt, teach and institute leadership. The aim of supervision should be to help people, do a better job. The supervision of management is in need of an overhaul as well as the supervision of production workers.

8. Drive out fear so that everyone may work effectively for the company. Create a climate of innovation.

9. Break down barriers between staff areas. People in research, design, sales and production must work as a team to foresee problems of production and use that may be encountered with the product or service. This open approach helps all of the employees to focus on the aims and purposes of the company.

10. Eliminate slogans, exhortations and targets for the work

force asking for zero defects and new levels of productivity.

11. Eliminate numerical quotas for the workforce and numerical goals for management and Management by Objectives. Instead, learn the capabilities of processes and how to improve them through leadership.

12. Remove barriers that rob people of pride of workmanship. The responsibility of supervisors must be changed from sheer numbers to quality. Eliminate the annual rating or merit system.

13. Institute a vigorous program of education and self-improvement for everyone.

14. Put everybody in the company to work to accomplish the transformation because the transformation is everyone's job.

Our mentor at the time, Marshall Thurber, started studying Deming in the late 70's. Even before learning of Deming's technology, he and Bobbi DePorter were committed to quality. After studying Deming's methods, he encouraged me, partners, and associates that led the logistical teams to create, implement, and fine-tune our systems.

Since then we have never stopped (and encourage all new partners, associates, and staff) to being committed to the constant, continuous improvement of the processes that make up all the parts of our organizations.

Because we actually use all the tools and principles we share throughout this *Money & You*™ *Book Series*, our work has been very successful – lasting longer than any other entrepreneurial, experiential, transformational education business globally. We are often referred to as *"The Rolls Royce of the seminar business."*

Unfortunately, many managers have never been trained or have any awareness of Deming's *Theory of Profound Knowledge* or our teachings and are simply unaware of its importance. They must first become aware of the value that systems like this have and how to constantly improve them in their organizations. Many people (entrepreneurs, professionals, teachers, students) get this awareness after attending our programs.

The Systems We Use:

The following are some examples of systems that we use in our organizations – they illustrate how to create powerful processes:

Policies: The key systems that run our company are documented in our *Policies* – a document entitled *Rules of the Game*. Everyone agrees to follow these policies when they work with our organization in just about any position – we live by them.

This was the number one tool that supported the extraordinary results of the organization that our work comes from... and it has continued to prove its power and effectiveness for nearly four decades in our organization alone.

I personally added the last two policies after I inherited the intellectual rights to the work in 1985. You can see the influence of the legal system in the 11th rule. This has become one of the most important policies for many not only in business but also in personal relationships including marriage, family and with children.

You can find the link to the Bonus Webinar on the *Rules of the Game* at http://www.MoneyandYou.com/Book – If you cannot find the link send an e-mail to our team and someone will help you: info@moneyandyou.com

If you look at the most successful companies and organizations in the world, they all have some version of the *Rules of the Game*.

Here they are for your use:

RULES OF THE GAME

Money & You® *Program*

1. Be willing to support our purposes, games, rules and goals.

2. Speak supportively.

3. Acknowledge whatever is being communicated as true for the speaker at that moment.

4.   Complete your agreements:

   a) Make only agreements that you are willing and intend to keep.

   b) Communicate any broken agreement(s) at the first appropriate time.

   c) Clear up any broken agreement at the first appropriate opportunity.

5. If a problem arises, first look to the system for corrections and then communicate your solution to the person who can do something about it.

6. Be effective and efficient (Optimize every event ... more with less).

7. Have the willingness to win and to allow others to win (win/win).

8. Focus on what works.

9. When in doubt, check your intuition.

10. Be responsible - no lay blame or justification.

11. Hold the person "innocent" until proven "guilty."

12. If an upset lasts longer than 50 minutes, the upset party(s) to seek support from a neutral third party.

©2015

Meeting Systems and Tools:

Upon being hired as employees or work with us as independent contractors, everyone learns that all staff meetings are a *"safe space"* for communications. We even have a system for communication if an upset is needed to be resolved amongst the company members.

People need to be listened to even if they are expressing a different opinion. If there is no safe environment in which to communicate, people will either shut down, or the stronger personality styles will dominate every meeting – this will cause breakdowns.Getting everyone's real opinion is vital to cohesive teamwork. This is a realistic measure of the effectiveness of the *Communications System* a company uses.

We always include a simple process at the beginning of our programs, or anytime team members are in the same location – plus, when necessary throughout the day – and it completes the day for the team – it's called the *What I Feel Like Saying (WIFLS)* process.

This process allows everyone to speak whatever is on their minds. The reason it's done at the beginning of a meeting (or a workday) is so that everyone gets "present"; plus, if there are any upsets, questions or considerations, it gets out of the person's mind into the open and whatever is said, can be acknowledged and let go of; if necessary it can be scheduled to be handled later.

Everyone gets to participate by stating whatever they feel like saying without interruption. It is like the tradition of having a "talking stick." The one holding the stick may say whatever they want, and everyone else must remain silent until they get the stick, and it is their turn to speak.

In addition to the daily meeting processes, these other systems are very useful and should be carefully customized to meet your needs. They are all explained in much more detail in the *Money-Making Systems Manual – For People Who Work With People*:

Memo System	Memos are communications put in writing in a three-part form to ensure clarity and follow-up. In this day and age, this system is transforming itself into interactive e-mails, texts/SMS's, Instant Messaging (IM) or other systems like WeChat, WhatsApp. The core tenant: **put your requests in writing**!
Office System	The layout of an office can minimize traffic flow and other interruptions.
Phone System	Designed to make forwarding calls to the right person easily and efficiently. This can now extend to text/SMS, IM, and other platforms already mentioned.
Web System	To make access to information easy and, people more productive – again through e-mail and other Web-based platforms as mentioned above.
Accounting System	Makes the inflow and outflow of money easily tracked and accessible to the management team and accountants for forecasting, projections, budgeting, and cash flow analysis.
Statistics System	Takes out the mystery out of the efficiency of your people and your business. Knowing what activities are being done, by whom, and not only how, but how many times. This gives clarity to what is actually being sold; what transactions are being done. **Statistics give you the facts on the business as opposed to opinions.**
Interpersonal Communications System	These are the processes or activities for starting meetings that allow people to begin to share openly and truthfully about what going on with them such as the *What I Feel Like Saying* process. It helps to clear the air and get people to be fully present in the moment.

The Importance of Open Communications:

The *What I Feel Like Saying* (WIFLS) process described earlier is the least used tools by companies and organizations, yet it is the most important. What most organizations don't realize is that 94% of the communications that occur between individuals are invisible. Only 6% of communications are verbal.

When people are allowed to verbalize their feelings in a safe environment negative energy disappears. Each issue can be dealt with and resolved; otherwise, it hangs in the space, and it can affect the members of the organization that are involved in the upset; plus, it breeds gossip.

Another powerful principle we use is *"correction without invalidation."* This is when team members communicate in a way so that it doesn't invalidate any comment or communication made by anyone. We all spend two-thirds of our lives at work... Who likes to be made wrong all day by people who think differently than you do?

Telling people to be innovative rarely works. You must build an atmosphere of innovation, experimentation and risk which is supported by a genuine desire to create a safe space for people to learn and reflect on what they are doing. One of the huge misconceptions about innovation is that it is all about the generation of ideas. In fact, that is only one small part of the challenge.

You must make sure that the ideas which are generated are then dispersed and shared with the people who are affected by them or who would want to know. It is only then that the process of discovery and improvement begins to reap benefits.

There is much to be studied about the *Deming technology* as well as other technologies. We hope that we gave you a small taste of Deming's and the brilliance of the powerful people systems that we have generated through the decades.

You might want to determine the gap in the effectiveness of your own organization's Personal Communications Systems, if any.

Feel free to use this list from the *Flight of the Buffalo* and make note of any gaps in your own policies and practices:

1. Do we have a coach/facilitator for empowering the human relations in each department?
2. Are all transactions between team members characterized by caring and integrity?
3. Do all the people in our company know how well they've done before they go home every night?
4. Do people have problems with other team members that they are avoiding?
5. Are the leaders constantly engaged in the challenge of learning to be a different leader?
6. Does our company encourage open communications in our staff meetings?
7. Are we encouraged to make mistakes and learn from them?
8. Is each person encouraged to ask, "what's the worse thing that can happen and how can I handle it"?
9. Can people authentically communicate why they do what they do?
10. Can people share what their anger is telling them what they need to learn about themselves?
11. Do they ask, "what am I doing about it"?
12. Do they ask others, "Am I stubborn with my customers or other team members"?
13. Can they "hear" the answer or do they justify, lay blame, or maintain a righteous attitude?
14. Do we ask here "How can we use this problem to stimulate learning about what it takes to be successful"?
15. Do we see "endings" as "beginnings" because of the way we handle our conflicts?

Many thanks to Marshall Thurber that as a Deming's technology expert shared with us much of this knowledge. Thanks also to all the other experts whose work is making a difference in the quality of life for many at work.

There are many effective systems from masters like W. Edwards

Deming, Jim Collins (*Good To Great* is one of the best business books I have ever read!) and others experts – too many to mention whose work contribute to the field of professional and organizational development. Through this book series, I will continue to introduce you to those that have made a tremendous contribution to us and many of our graduates.

To reinforce our message... what they all seem to be saying is: *"Put systems in to run your business, but remember to also put the 'heart' into your relationships."* This is the way to long-term, lasting results. We know from our own experience that when the "heart" is missing, so is the effortless joy, success, and productivity in business...

Please take the time to study and apply the many systems that we are introducing to you – the results will positively surprise you!

Chapter 4 – In Review

1. **If you set up the system to support your people,** your people will give you what you want.
2. **A system is self-correcting and duplicable**; it is stable - predictable within a certain range of variation.
3. **Deming** said, *"94% of failures in business outcomes are <u>systems</u> failures."*
4. **Systems We Use:**
    a. All the systems that run our company are documented in our Policies.
    b. Meeting Systems - All staff meetings are a "safe space" for communications - even if it is an argument that is needed to work through something.
5. **Basic Systems:**
    a. Memo System
    b. Office Layout System
    c. Phone System
    d. Web System
    e. Accounting System
    f. Statistics System
    g. Interpersonal Communications Systems

Chapter 5

Aligned Teams

The systems just shared in the last chapter are key to creating aligned teams... Aligning teams is a big subject! Once you master this important subject, leveraging your products, services (and gifts) will be much easier!

This chapter will give you even further distinctions that will empower you to become a better leader, business owner or manager – even a better team player!

To repeat this key point: people are like "little packages" of feelings, emotions, thoughts and prejudices. They may not know what it took for you to get to where you are, your past learning experiences and what has been going on in your business before they got there. They may even make assumptions. And without asking why you do what you do, some may think that they know more about business than you do – especially about your business – so they think that they can just come in and hit the ground running. In their opinion, they have great ideas and can see ways of running your business infinitely better than the way you are running it.

You can always tell when someone has been in business or management for a considerable time. They share "war stories" and experiences with other business owners and managers. They don't make them wrong – nor tell them how to do things the "*right*" or "*their way.*"

As a business owner (or manager) you can save everyone a lot of time and energy – not to mention speculation – by letting your staff know *why* you are in business. Tell them what you personally and emotionally get out of providing your product or service to your clients and customers. In other words, tell them your "big why."

And then discover their "big why" they are working with you. besides just earning a living...

To empower them further, do the following...

Financial Goals For Your Team Members:

One of the first things to know is what your team members need to handle their "survival." Don't hire people that are in need of a higher income. If they are potentially a very valued team member – or their financial situation has changed for some reason – and your organization cannot pay the income that they need to provide for their families or personal goals, you may want to discuss their long-term goals and help them look for other available options within the organization to provide for their basic needs.

Here are some questions that can be asked:

- Could they work on a flexible time schedule so that they could have another job?

- Could you all earn more if a certain goal is reached by the business within a certain amount of time?

- Are there opportunities for employees who would like to earn more? Could they sell your product or service outside of their normal job and generate additional commissions for themselves?

- Could you tap into the rich network of the people in your employees' sphere of influence? Remember that every person knows at least 200 people... the networking power of the people who work for you alone could be staggering! What are the resources in their personal circle of friends, family and past business relationships? If you do not ask, you will not know.

As you discover what works for you, your organization and the people who want to work with you, you may find that they may want to work for you more for the *learning experience* than for their direct financial rewards.

There's life-long benefit when one applies for jobs because of what one can *learn* as opposed as to what one can *earn*. Discuss this option openly, from the beginning, with your people. If they agree, create rules of the game how this can be accomplished, the expectations and the commitment. This can be a very beneficial arrangement for all.

There are two things to remember:

1. **Have clear agreements** to protect you and prevent people from going into competition with you.

2. **Include those you employ** in your discussions about their financial requirements and options as well as yours.

Other Money-Related Issues:

Assumption of a Company's Profit: Team members have been known to develop resentment towards a business owner if they have made unrealistic assumptions about how much money the business is making and compare it to what they are earning.

Inexperienced people may sometimes get a glimpse of income ledgers or assume they know how profitable the company is by calculating the gross revenues of the business based on what they can see. But unless they know all the actual operating costs, meaning, have they ever had to scramble to make payroll, they can never understand what the real bottom line is.

For example, in our educational company, it is natural for people to mentally estimate the number of people in a program, multiply that number times the amount of the tuition and assume the owners are making a lot of money. But of course, they have failed to calculate a few of the costs involved:

1. The costs of learning by experience what we are teaching.

2. R&D costs of program content, hiring of experts, testing of the curriculum.

3. Staff salaries to promote and prepare for the event.
4. Enrollment and registration costs.
5. Royalties or licensing fees for training materials, printing costs, etc.
6. Training and costs of developing and bringing your sales team (or promoters) up to speed until you are not required to be present; and they can match your level of professionalism, image and sales results needed to make the enterprise profitable.
7. Direct promotion and advertising costs. Web costs.
8. Office supplies for the promotion and marketing of the event.
9. Logistical supplies for the events.
10. Sales costs and commissions.
11. Instructor's / Program director's fees or salaries.
12. Travel costs for the instructor(s)/Program director(s).
13. Legal expenses for contracts, agreements, insurance.
14. Costs for the venue (including non-refundable deposits and guarantees for events that may be canceled for any reason).
15. Food and refreshments for participants / logistical staff — and the staff to handle it.

And there are always unexpected costs during events. As you can see, the team would have a very different picture after understanding these expenses in advance. It's key to educate your team and have a true understanding of the bottom-line profitability of the business.

Share Your Vision:

Business studies have shown that *money* is NOT most people's number one priority or objective in their job. Much to many people's surprise is that more than money, what ranks higher in value to most people is:

- *Being included in decisions that will affect them*
- *Being asked their opinion*
- *Being paid attention to with respect*
- *Management doing what they say they are going to do*
- *Being acknowledged for their contribution on a regular basis*

Sure you can hire anyone with the lure of money, but how do you keep them motivated? How do you keep them happy, honest and not tempted to step out and become your competition?

Brightness of the Future:

Share where you plan to take the company – your *"brightness of the future"* – including what you want for your people and what possibilities it provides for everyone who participates and supports the organization in reaching its vision, mission, and goals.

When you share your vision and how your business fits your personal purpose, others can see how their own purpose might align with yours and the organization's.

They could begin to see a bigger purpose for being part of your organization that is worth much more than the money they make. Plus, the awareness that contributing to you with their time, dedication and energy could create profits, fulfillment and a sense of contribution, could be very exciting for them...

This is what will keep them working with you, being faithful and trustworthy. When your team members get that their own sense of purpose is being fulfilled by being part of your business, they will happily stay and produce extraordinary results for you... This is also true for associates, affiliates – and even suppliers!

What is a Vision, Purpose, and Mission?

For a company or business, a **vision** is a picture of what they intend to be; a description of the "essence" of the environment and the "feeling tone" that will be felt in the business. A "Vision Statement" might contain references to how the company intends to make that future into a reality.

A **vision** does not necessarily have to have a huge humanitarian component – one that you are going to save the world. It can be simple and "paint a picture" that can be easily understood. It may be about how your clients and team (and those that you touch) will benefit from your products or services and the environment that will be created.

A Vision Statement can incorporate:

- A financial or service outcome you would like to achieve through the work your company does.
- Having your company be the fastest growing company in your area.
- Having it be the one that produces the best of whatever it is you do.
- Having the happiest team members whom will someday share in the profits, and revenue stream, that you all produce together.
- Having everyone who works with you finally enjoy a higher standard of living, or be able to contribute to others because of his or her association with you.

As I shared earlier, the **vision** that we live by and was given to us by our beloved mentor, Bucky Fuller: *How do we make the world work for 100% of humanity in the shortest possible time, through spontaneous cooperation, without ecological offense or disadvantage of anyone?* That is such a wonderful example of a vision!

A **purpose** is a statement that keeps you and your team inspired; and it communicates to your clients or customers, suppliers and all those that may support your work, the "essence of the work" – the "reason" for your organization.

The purpose of our organization is: *To Uplift Humanity's Consciousness Through Socially-Responsible Businesses.* We added the "socially-responsible" distinction in the past ten years since there was a greater understanding and acceptance of that term.

Our purpose evolved through the decades. The purpose of what turned out to be my work was designed when I first attended the *Burklyn Business School for Entrepreneurs* – it was designed by my class in a three-day process – *Self-Actualization Through Profitable Business*. As an organization, we also used *World Peace Through Business*. And in the '80's we even had a slogan that I still love and it's so appropriate at moments: *Trust the Dance*. That is not a purpose... and it's great inspiration at rough moments!

As you can see, your purpose, vision, and mission evolve as you do!

Finally, while a Vision Statement might contain references as to how the company intends to make that future into a reality, the "how" is part of the **Mission**.

One of our missions is: *to transform educational systems around the world and eradicate poverty and hunger.*

Organizations like ours that have a socially-responsible component to it and our mission is to add value to humanity, we find it very useful to share our vision, purpose, and mission on our Social Media platforms, promotional materials and in our marketing. This supports us in identifying the type of person that we want to attract to our work. You can do the same.

If you are just starting to build an organization, sit down and work out a vision that you can all relate to, with your partners or team. If you work alone, get support from friends that are familiar with the concept.

Either way, it's a great driving force, and it will support your marketing, finding good people, keeping your spirits high and taking you through rough times. A simple but yet powerful tool...

Owner's Life Style:

One problem that can occur if the business owners or managers flaunt an extravagant lifestyle – driving expensive cars, wearing expensive jewelry and clothing – is that people in the organization may resent them. Of course, everyone deserves to have beautiful things, especially if you have been working on your business for many years.

We recommend that you explain to your team your own goals and the little or big "extravagances" that your business now allows you to have. Help them appreciate the investment that you have made, long before they joined you; the years of sacrifice, the stretching that you (and possibly your family) have done to this point, and the discipline it has taken you to get to where you are today.

People love to celebrate success. It becomes a model of possibility for them to follow. But they cannot appreciate what the sacrifices that it may have taken you unless you share. So rather than flaunt it and have them make up their own stories, tell them the facts.

Any time clear communication is lacking, you can expect people to become upset and resentful. This is why we so highly recommend an open communication policy and regular *What I Feel Like Saying* sessions.

When in Doubt, Ask… then Listen.

If you think about it, the job of a manager or business owner is to make sure their people succeed at work; and each employee's job is to make sure their manager wins. Ask people what would make their jobs better or easier for them. Ask what they need in order to their tasks faster, better and more efficiently.

People love to be asked for their opinions and will freely give them to you if you ask. What you do with the information is up to you; however, we highly recommend that you LISTEN ACTIVELY. If necessary, repeat back to them what you think they just said or ask clarifying questions, then take their useful recommendations and put them into action. These are the steps that will create continuous improvement of your organization.

By the way, this is different from what I mentioned before about people liking to tell you what to do. You don't have to take every suggestion people make to try to change your business, but you should ask people AFTER they have been working YOUR system for awhile what they see and what they may need to do a better job. This is especially beneficial considering the speed at which new technology is becoming available.

This act of asking and listening allows your people to know that you are interested in their input. If something they suggest is a good idea but not affordable now, ask them how they could help to earn it as a reward either individually or as a team. Who said all the sales people worked in the sales and marketing department? Who said the engineers can only work in the "back of the shop"?

This is what Deming was   constantly recommending – that the people on the ground are the best quality controllers and will have the best input.

Tips for Alignment and Preventing Upsets:

1. Have clear financial goals for your business or organization.
2. Help your team members and associates develop their own clear financial goals.
3. Anticipate when you think they will be able to reach their own goals, especially if in the beginning, the business is not able to provide what they need.
4. Determine if people can or are willing to contribute to the business' overall success by investing their own time, energy or even money – perhaps in the form of delayed payments until the business gets going on its own. In exchange, of course, they would get a specified return on the profits.

Some of these suggestions may be uncomfortable to handle at first; however, when you do handle these important issues properly, you will have an easier and smoother running business. Your team will be more focused and happier, working towards common goals that they understand and are on board with.

Listen To Your Gut:

When you follow the suggestions outlined in this book, you are automatically creating an environment where trust and personal integrity has a place to live and is experienced by everyone; therefore, it is important to deal with, or confront, any issues or subjects that give you an uneasy feeling or a knot in the pit of your stomach when you think of them.

Trust your "inner wisdom." It is seldom misleading. Bring up and address unsettling issues with whoever is involved. If you do not confront and deal with those uncomfortable issues immediately, they could "fester" and become really uncomfortable problems later on. People know energetically when something is "out of sorts." Most people will appreciate you candidly sharing what is bothering you because it almost always will be bothering them as well.

If people are holding out on their emotional authenticity or if they are playing "judge and jury" and they are not willing to engage in open, authentic discussion from the heart, then they probably are not contributing positive energy to your team anyway. Perhaps they need to be working elsewhere.

What Are You Willing To Support?

Are you doing as much as you can to support the people whose work leverages you? When you leverage yourself through others, get clear on what you are willing to do to support them. Find out what they need and want. Look around your business today. Set aside time for company planning events or retreats to discuss these issues.

If you do not know where to start or how to determine what people need, ask them. Most people will tell you what they need, especially if you have set up the type of work environment where people are free to contribute to the overall success of the company.

How to tell if you are doing a good job in this area... Ask yourself:

- Do your people get to go to training programs like sales seminars or programs related to their job? Web or Social Media trainings are key in certain businesses. Personal growth classes periodically can also be very beneficial. In my world, they are absolutely essential for the leader (and manager(s)) to ensure the success of the organization.

- Do you buy them special equipment, computers, and programs, as they need them, so that these tools will make their work easier, faster or more efficient?

- Do you upgrade your communications systems with accessories like great headsets, or provide the proper ergonomically designed chairs and desks that can make the difference to someone who is on the phone or on a computer all day?

- Are your offices pleasant, well lit and conducive to a comfortable work environment?

- Do people feel like they can ask for what they need?

Or are you of a mindset that a work environment is not supposed to be pleasant and that people should struggle – perhaps because you had to struggle at first? Do people have to "earn the right" to enjoy a high quality of work life? Are you the type of person that thinks, "I'll give them what they need AFTER they prove to me they deserve it"? Food for thought!

Learn Their Natural Motivators:

To learn what motivates each person you meet, we recommend having everyone take their own DISC Personal Profile when you hire them as well as when you promote them into a different level of leadership. DISC graphs in the reports and the textual descriptions identify their primary style which then tells the DISC-literate person as to what naturally motivates them.

Each style has very different needs, emotions, and fears that motivate each behavioral style. DISC is based on a universal language which names the patterns of each different style and their focus – *Dominance of Problems*, *Influence of People*, *Steadiness of the Pace of the Environment*, or *Compliance of the Procedures and rules that give consistency in results*.

We feel it is everyone's job to learn how to recognize and relate to the "observable behaviors" everyone sees when they meet. A team leader that knows how to interact most appropriately with each of the styles will find it easy to create an aligned team that gets consistent results:

- **For the High D's,** give them the authority to **Control** the "big picture" situation – like how to improve on the competition or how to manage the company within the current economy, trends, culture, etc.

- **With the High I's** who love **Influencing** other to work with them to get the job done faster or better, give them opportunities to collaborate and work with other people to do it. Give them a few minutes of social talk before getting down to business and acknowledge them in front of others. They'll love it and do that much more to keep earning the praise.

- **Your High S's** love supporting the team and instinctively know how to create the types of systems that **Steady** *the pace of the* environment. For them, it is all about making it easier for others to work with ease, so appreciate their incredible patience and ability to listen – without interruption! Take an active interest in them and don't rush into the agenda too fast.

- **High C's** work best when they have clarity on what you want so they can focus on ensuring high quality and correctness. They want to make sure everyone in the company is **Complying** with the procedures, policies, and rules that are in place. Be aware of this need when delegating a task to them because it is not something High D's and I's instinctively do!

Once you know which person has which motivators, you can watch for these important opportunities to keep them motivated and make you a better manager:

- **Give your High D's lots of independence, authority, and control over the way they do things.** Make any presentation brief. Ask and give them bottom line statements and answers.

Follow up to ensure they are satisfied with the solution, and get out of their way once you have given them a problem to solve or a project to do!

- **Give your High I's other people to interact with – ideally who will give and positive recognition of their achievements.** Give them the big picture and let them talk things over with you first before having to write a report. High I's are always appreciative of the attention you give them, so alternate questions between them personally and in business. Provide incentives for making decisions and show how the solutions enhance their image or saves them effort.

- **Provide your S's with the opportunity to set up their own systems** (if yours are not efficient). Present new ideas in a non-threatening way. They love predictability and the sense of stability and the security that things won't change too fast. When change is imminent, give them plenty of time to think about it and adjust. Provide consistent follow-up with personal assurances.

- **Provide your High C's clear instructions, time requirements and structure.** Skip the small talk but ask questions that reveal their expertise. Provide logical options with documentation. Fill them in with details that assure them that quality is important to you and appreciate their extra effort in making sure their work is done correctly, accurately and completely.

If you take the time to show your people you understand and care about their needs, they will automatically give you more than what you ask for. Invest in the little things that make life better for your people and you will create a working environment that is inviting to come to every day.

When the original creator of my *Money & You*® program, Marshall Thurber, and his partners set up their real estate development company in San Francisco that salvaged beautiful Victorian mansions – and created a fortune in that niche – they were using the *Excellerated Business*

Success Model being taught in this book. At that time this title had not been given to the model – it wasn't until years later when someone asked Marshall to describe the key principles to creating a successful business that he summarized the model in this manner... brilliant!

For instance, when the policies piece in the *Team Alignment* process that has been described in this chapter was put in place, they actually had to put in a policy *requiring* people to take at least one day off a week. With their flexible work time policies, open communication environment and bottom line incentives in profit sharing bonuses, people were so motivated and happy to be there, they would rather be at work than go home!

Do you think they had any problems with productivity and creating profits? Not at all!

Delegate Responsibility to Your Team:

One of the most important distinctions in being able to leverage and duplicate yourself is to **master delegation**.

Some people think that *to delegate* means to simply get rid of work they don't want to do. Not true. Real delegation is not turning it over because, in the end, you are still accountable for the result. Rather, it is empowering others in order to create the leverage.

Delegation Strategies:

The following strategies will help you to free yourself from being the typical "lone-ranger" or "do it all yourself" business owner or executive. These are the things that also could cripple your potential for success, especially if you are a *High S or C* that thinks no one else could possibly do it as well as you could! (As a *Hi C* myself, I can confirm that they can't :-) but you have to leverage!)

And by the same token, *High D's and I's* should not try "to be everything to everybody either!" Encourage everyone to learn what the styles are of others in their teams.

No one likes to work with people who are "bottlenecks" in the flow of productive activities in a business. They won't let go of things that other people could do for them, so the business suffers.

1. Take the risk:

Give a new assignment to someone who is less experienced and who has the potential for development. It is tempting to give work to your most experienced person because there is no sense of risk. You know that the senior person can do the task. Instead, even though it may seem risky at first, you may be surprised at the hidden talents you uncover. An added bonus is that it may help them feel better about you!

2. Be prepared:

We are not suggesting that you give an assignment to someone who is not ready for it. If you do, the project may be doomed to fail. First ask yourself: *"Are they adequately trained for the job?"* *"Do they have access to the correct information?"* *"Can they operate the necessary equipment?"* Bottom line, *"Are they prepared?"* If not, give them an experienced person to work with, the training they need or other growth and development opportunities. It may be that they just need more self-confidence or assertiveness training. Don't forget the *C's* will be hesitant to take on a new assignment unless the instructions are clear, and their risk of failure is low. The *S's* will be willing, but may put more time and effort into it than you'd like, keeping them from other work that may be more suitable for the gifts of their style.

3. Be patient:

Allow adequate time for a person to fully understand the assignment and complete it. Be reasonable with your demands.

Do not give a novice a budget report to do and expect it in half a day. (Remember how long it took you the first time you learned a new skill? Did you make a lot of mistakes?) Remember, making mistakes is the natural way people learn.

The key to learning is to *make mistakes*, then correct without invalidation.

4.   **Do not breathe down their necks:**

Once you've delegated the assignment, carefully explained the requirements and set the deadlines (and had them repeat back to you what they heard you want to be done) then leave them to it. Constant monitoring not only hinders performance, but it can also create a sense of inadequacy. Give people a reasonable amount of independence and let them prove their abilities. While it takes longer in the beginning, this investment of time will pay handsome dividends.

5.   **Delegate the authority:**

When you delegate responsibility without also giving the person the authority to carry it out, you are creating a no-win situation. Someone's ability to do the job effectively depends a great deal on the powers you allow them to exercise. Always establish the parameters of authority. Be clear on who makes what decisions. If you do not hand over any real authority for decisions around the project, all you'll get is someone willing to do the work but unable to carry it out fully.

6.   **Spell out what you want:**

There is no sense in delegating work to someone who does not fully grasp what you are after. Make sure your instructions are understandable by having people repeat your instructions back to you in their own words. Set clear parameters and expectations and check back in with them often enough so that you are confident they are not getting frustrated.

7.   **In search of perfection:**

The "perfectionist" in you can strike when least expected and may foil all of your well-laid delegation plans. Break the perfection habit! Recognize this particularly if YOU have high *S* and/or *C* tendencies. (We know no one can really do it as <u>well</u> as *you* can; however, give them a chance!) You may be able to do the job better or faster, but you are now going to be concentrating on *Income Generating Activities*. Do not get in the way of the overall progress of your business!

Remember – out there somewhere is a person who can do it just as well as you. You may have to accept a few mistakes along the way but just grit your teeth and bear it. It is a fact that *"you'll never build an empire while you're still making the bricks yourself!"*

IN SUMMARY – TO GAIN THE MOST FROM YOUR TEAM AS AN ENTREPRENEUR:

- **It is your objective to delegate yourself out of a job** so that you can move upward and onward to your next venture.
- **Determine what can you delegate** so you can start working ON your business, not IN it.
- **Allow others to make mistakes** to learn and gain from correcting them. Then, just like you, someday they will master their own area of interest. It just takes time...

Chapter 5 – In Review

1. **Have a vision worked out from the beginning.**

2. **Ask what makes the job better** or easier for your employees. Listen actively – take some of their recommendations and implement them.

3. **Share Your Vision With Your Employees**
    1. Include them in decisions that will affect them.
    2. Ask their opinion.
    3. Pay attention with respect.

4. **Listen to Your Gut**

5. **Get clear** about what you are willing to do to support those leveraging you.

6. **If you take time** to show your people you understand and care about their needs, they'll automatically give more than asked for.

7. **Delegation Strategies:**
    a. Take the Risk
    b. Be Prepared
    c. Be Patient
    d. Do not breathe down their necks
    e. Delegate the Authority
    f. Spell out what you want
    g. In search of "Perfection"

Chapter 6

Synergy

Synergy has been a popular word in business and management circles for decades now. I am not sure whether most people really understand it or have had the ability to recognize it when they have had an *experience* of synergy in their lives or business. It's one of those words that is loosely used but not quite comprehended.

One dictionary's definition of synergy is *"the cooperative action of discrete agencies such that the total effect is greater than the sum of the effects taken independently."*

Our *Burklyn Business School* instructor, mentor, and friend, Bucky Fuller, originally coined this word. He explained (to us personally and in many of his publications) that in studies and work with metals and minerals, metallurgists would find that when certain metals were combined, their strength was far greater than what could have been expected by computing the known strength of each individual component. It was from this example that he got the concept of *synergy*.

In looking at nature, Bucky uncovered what he called "generalized principles" that are always true without exception. He said, *"when there is synergy, people working together create unexpected results because their efforts actually create a third energy that is only present with this particular combination."* Here's a great site set up by our *Money & You*® graduate and friend, Peter Meisen where you can learn more about Bucky's generalized principles: http://www.meetup.com/Buckminster-Fuller-Generalized-Principles-4-Living-Success/

We see fantastic examples of *synergy* in the news in the form of heroic endeavors, or when a group of people achieves incredible results because they are completely aligned towards a specific goal. In this equation one plus one no longer equals two, it equals 11...

When *synergy* is experienced, it is common to have unexpected and extraordinary results. Because the results are unexpected, some people may call it a "miracle." Whatever you call it, when there is *synergy*, the result is greater than anyone could have expected.

How To Create Synergy:

Synergy is most likely to be created purposefully when you apply the systems, follow the generalized principles and distinctions we've discussed in this book.

This includes learning from the experience of **Masters** who have gone before you; creating a **Niche** that fills a need no one is filling; getting the right people, in the right jobs, to run your system; creating **Leverage** by building an **Aligned Team** through **Systems** which creates **Alignment** by having clear plans of action, policies, procedures and *Rules of the Game* which will get **Results...** Piece of cake!

In other words, the most successful small and large businesses and organizations all have those important elements in common.

And because I am a *Hi C* and have been implementing these tools for so long, I know that it would be beneficial for some of you for me to summarize these elements in another way:

These organizations are clear on their:

- Vision, purpose, mission
- Goals
- Policies/Rules of the Game
- Systems for empowering their people
- Personality types
- Organizational Charts
- Clear lines of communications
- Job Descriptions
- Operations Manuals
- Their leaders are committed to having a learning organization

When you learn how to delegate and share your vision so that others are inspired to find their vision in your work, the chances of your team creating synergy are greatly enhanced; and the success, profitability and joy in your business will exceed your dreams.

Discover a product or service that is needed and wanted and provide it for a profit... and if you can add value to humanity in the process, now we are rocking!

The promise of entrepreneurship being able to transform this world to work for 100% of humanity is one step closer because of YOU!

Chapter 6 – In Review

1. **True synergy** is when the result of cooperation is greater than anyone could have expected. One plus one is not two, it's 11.

2. **How to Create Synergy** – be are clear on your:
    - Vision, purpose, mission
    - Goals
    - Policies/Rules of the Game
    - Systems for empowering their people
    - Personality types
    - Organizational Charts
    - Clear lines of communications
    - Job Descriptions
    - Operations Manuals and be committed to having a learning organization!

"Every human being is ruled by the law of habit. Because this is true, the person who learns to build his habits to order practically controls the major cause of successful achievement."

Napoleon Hill

Chapter 7

Results

You don't have success if you don't have the results to show for it. As a wonderful mentor, Marcia Martin, taught me long ago, **in life you have either reasons or results.** Reasons why you didn't create what you've wanted or results that speak for themselves!

If you don't create the results that you want in business, go back over this list:

1.   Be clear on your personal purpose.

Why did you go into that project or business originally? What was the purpose? If you do something for x-length of time just to make money, so you could contribute later, that is fine. Just be clear on your purpose.

2.   Be clear on your goals:

a.   Be sure to have very clear goals.
b.   Have anything that is in the way of you reaching your goals CLEARED away.

3.   Clear blocks to having results.

a.   Clear any emotional or stumbling blocks that you may be in the way.
b.   How well can you communicate who you are and what you are about?

4. **If you can't reach the goals you want, get personal support.**

    a.   Find a Master that can support you.

    b.   Tell them what you meant to do and where you got stopped.

    c.   They can often see what you can't about what went wrong.

    d.   Be sure to discover what you could have done to leverage yourself.

    e.   Personal support and mentors are critical in overcoming your own "make me wrong" inner talk. It is that voice in your head that tells you that you should have done it better.

    f.   Acknowledge the mistakes you have made. Get personal support from someone you can trust and determine how to overcome issues in the future.

    h.   DO A LIST OF YOUR MISTAKES AROUND MONEY, FINANCES AND LEARNING EXPERIENCES IN BUSINESS, and write A RESPONSE COLUMN. Notice the little voice in your head and what it is telling you about those mistakes. The intent is to get these old thoughts out of your subconscious. You then create a positive statement to overcome that negative conditioning.

    In my *Access to Cash* book in this series, there's a whole chapter entitled *"Magical Exercises"* that has a powerful and proven step-by-step process on how to clear blocks to creating results and negative decisions about money, business, and success.

5. **Reward Yourself**

    a.   Set small goals and celebrate.

    b.   Reward yourself for mistakes instead of making self-wrong.

    c.   The bigger the mistake, the bigger the gift.

    d.   Ask "How do I really want my life to be?" Are you living it?

6. **Be Disciplined**

    a.   Be a "disciple" of your higher self – of your inner knowing.

b.   We only experience others as we experience ourselves.

c   If you say you are going to do something, and you don't accomplish that result, your subconscious may hold you "guilty" and consider it a "broken agreement" with yourself and not allow you to win in the future. Important to clear any decisions made.

d.   Discipline is key to creating magnificent results!

7.   Study People Who Have Created Results In Your Field

Keep learning and expanding. Ask them what they have done to create results in their lives

8.   Monitor Yourself

a.   Keep doing this all the time, especially with statistics so that you look at the facts – what you are really accomplishing... or not.

b.   Measure the time you are spending on "income-generating activities" i.e. how many sales call, etc.

c.   When you are doing well, don't change anything, keep doing it!

d.   Only change what you are not doing well.

9.   Keep learning!

REMEMBER: when all seems to fail, "GOD MAKES NO MISTAKES"... it may be that the "learning experience" that you are going through is going to save you more pain or loss in the future.

If you look back at your life, some of the toughest lessons led you to have more distinctions, discernment and the ability to see more accurately at business situations and how to best create results. The key is to take action and keep going!

Chapter 7 – In Review

1.   Be clear on your personal purpose.

2.   Be clear on your goals.

3.   Clear the blocks to have any results.

4.   If you can't reach the goals you want, get personal support.

5.   Reward yourself.

6.   Be disciplined.

7.   Study people who have created results in your field.

8.   Monitor yourself.

9.   Keep learning!

God Makes No Mistakes...

Chapter 8

In Summary

There are three words in (any language) that are most misunderstood – and though people use them freely and think they know the essence of their meaning – in actuality the only way to know the real meaning is to experience them by applying them, practicing them and creating results.

The words are: **systems, leverage, and love.**

This book has been about systems and leverage.

The by-product of applying systems and creating leverage is a loving environment where teams are willing to work around the clock for you, be faithful to your purpose and be willing to grow your business as if it were theirs. The business will be much more profitable!

The company members will be happier, they will go home more fulfilled and have a happier personal life. Happy people are people who have a tendency to be more loving. **The result is love all around**.

If you apply the systems shared, your team will come up with their own possibilities for profit-sharing plans that most likely will keep the members of your organization around for decades. That they will be faithful and "go to bat" for you anytime. A win/win environment will encourage innovation, creativity and forward-thinking – the ultimate insurance that will keep you ahead of the competition – and attract "hot players" in just about any industry.

These systems will encourage cooperation amongst your key team members, divisions, affiliates, and suppliers – all those that matter to you and the success of your business. Remember, you are either creating profits or saving in costs, which ultimately translates to success for you.

This is not a pipe dream – many have demonstrated that this works...!

You are now privy to one of the most successful models that have been used by millions around the globe in just about every industry – its application always creates extraordinary results.

You can use this *Excellerated Business Success Model* as a template from which to pattern your own successful venture, enterprise, team or organization. It can be applied in all types of businesses, industries or cultures – regardless of how long you have been in business or how many employees you have.

Once you are familiar with this model, you will start noticing that it is being applied (with variations) in almost every successful business and organization (whether for profit or not). They all incorporate versions of the key distinctions presented in this model.

This is why we teach it in our programs. We illustrate even more organizational distinctions in our *Money-Making Systems* manual, which you can customize to fit your own business, putting it into the culture and any context that you want to establish. You will see it demonstrated in many companies which names you would easily recognize.

Well-known companies are natural demonstrations of the effectiveness and applications of the principles we recommend include: *Starbucks, Ben and Jerry's Ice Cream, Paul Mitchell Hair Products, Facebook, Whole Foods, Toms Shoes,* and others. You will see excellence in all their systems, their high levels of employee satisfaction, their outstanding customer service departments; and in the exceptional quality of their products and services – and some are committed to the betterment of humanity. All this adds up to why they are so successful.

We have come full circle in describing the systems needed to reduce the "learning curve" and make it easy to succeed. So now the question is, *"How are you going to apply them and the Excellerated Business Success Model to your own business?"*

What systems will you put in place to make the *invisible, visible?* What *Business Success Model* will you use to create your legacy? Will you integrate these systems easily – or will you forget and just stay "stuck" and possibly losing market share rather than gaining it?

Final advice: Do not skip any of the steps in the model thinking that *other* people need this technology but not you. Just because you may have not heard of some of these specific systems before, doesn't mean that you do not need to apply them.

Even if you are not interested in making the world better, these management tools will support your organization in having happier, healthier and more productive people that will bring more profits for you!

MAKE IT <u>YOUR</u> MODEL — STARTING TODAY!

"I give thanks daily, not for more riches, but for the wisdom with which to recognize, embrace and properly use the great abundance of riches I now have at my command."

Napoleon Hill

About the Author

Dame DC Cordova is a CEO, Global Business Developer, a Sustainability Entrepreneur, an Ambassador of New Education, and Mentor of Nurturing. She owns the *Excellerated Business Schools® for Entrepreneurs, Money & You®* and other *Excellerated* programs. Her business is a global organization that has over 100,000 graduates from over 65 countries.

She and her team have had a profound influence in the Asian Pacific region and in North America. The programs are taught in English and Chinese. Dame DC Cordova is a successful Latin woman and is expanding her programs to be taught in Spanish and other languages. Many of today's most well-known wealth and business authors and trainers have attended Dame DC Cordova's *Money & You* programs. Her training has transformed the way they teach and run their organizations.

Through these graduates – including Robert T. Kiyosaki, the co-author of the best-selling book series, *Rich Dad/Poor Dad*, her business partner of 9 years – and their organizations, have touched the lives of millions all over the world. The essence of her work is to add value to humanity, not just focus on the bottom line.

Her stated purpose is to *"uplift humanity's consciousness through socially-responsible businesses."* Leading by example, she is a philanthropist and a humanitarian. DC (as she is affectionately known) is an *Ambassador of New Education*. DC is tireless in her pursuit to transform educational systems around the world and eradicate poverty and hunger. DC is a *Mentor of Nurturing*, through her work with high-level entrepreneurs and business leaders.

DC is now expanding her work to the renewable energy field. She's in partnership as the *Global Business Developer* with Huang Ming, a "billionaire with heart," and one of the world's leading solar architect. Huang Ming is a winner of the *Right Livelihood Award* (the alternative Nobel Prize). He built the first *Solar Valley* in the world in Dezhou, China – a city with over 7 million people that use solar power. Huang

Ming is responsible for the passing of the first green law in China: http://www.SolarValleyChina.com

She was part of the group of pioneers led by Marshall Thurber and Bobbi DePorter of http://www.SuperCamp.com that developed the transformational, experiential, entrepreneurial training industry. She inherited the work over three decades ago. Through countless partners, associates, teams, graduates and the support of many, she has grown a global organization through a licensing business model. Licensing her work has allowed her the independence to expand her business endeavors into renewable energy, other businesses and to continue her humanitarian efforts. She has reached this level of success by utilizing the many tools, principles and systems taught in the *Excellerated* programs and her numerous publications.

DC is one of the contributors to the book, *Think & Grow Rich for Women*. She is the co-author of the comprehensive systems manual, *Money-Making Systems – For People Who Work With People*. Best-selling authors ask her to be a contributor in and to write forewords for many of their books. DC is a sought-after speaker and has spoken on hundreds of stages, podcasts, teleseminars, summits and has participated in dozens of motivational films, TV, and Internet shows.

She is the author of the *Money & You*™ *Book Series,* which is designed to educate the masses with proven tools, systems, and distinctions used by millions to reach financial success and add value to humanity.

DC has been interviewed around the world, in every type of media and hosted the *Money & You*® Radio Show. She is active in many Social Media platforms and thoroughly enjoys keeping up with the latest technological marvels. She uses her skills to promote the dissemination of information that supports "a world that works for 100% of humanity."

She is driven to move the world from a paradigm of scarcity to sufficiency, thus creating abundant resources for all.

DC is a founding member of the *Transformational Leadership Council (TLC)* and the *Southern California Association of Transformational Leaders (ATL)*; a facilitator and contributor for the *Pachamama Alliance* organization; a member of the Australian entrepreneurial network, *Unstoppables*; a facilitator and ambassador for the *Shine Global* community; an international business development consultant for *Achievest / The Family Bank Game*; a global business development advisor for the *American Renewal Energy Institute (AREI);* the Asia Pacific development consultant and member of the board of advisors of *SuperLab*; the international business development advisor for *The California Women's Conference*; *Spiritual Godmother* for *Heart of All Women*, a Silicon Valley Social Enterprise Start-up.

She supports numerous non-profits, foundations, and humanitarian organizations as mentor and champion. Most recently DC created the *Humanitarian Mastermind Series*. This program is designed to educate humanitarians around the world with powerful and proven business and organizational tools.

On her birthday, Nov. 14, 2010, DC was Knighted as *Dame of Honor* by *The Sovereign Order of the Orthodox Knights Hospitaller of Saint John of Jerusalem* – name changed to: *Orthodox Order of St. John Russian Grand Priory* (the oldest Humanitarian Order in the world) for her lifelong service to humanity. On January 2013, she was advanced to *Dame Commander of Grace* for her contribution to the growth of the Order: http://oosj-rgp.org/

More Information
Organizations & Resources

Dame DC Cordova:
http://www.DCCordova.com
http://www.MoneyandYou.com/Book (Bonus Materials)

Download Free 4-Session Business Make-Over — 4 hours of Entrepreneurial education: http://www.MoneyandYou.com

Money-Making Systems Manual & On-line Course to "excellerate" your entrepreneurial skills; step-by-step office / desk organization
http://www.MoneyandYou.com/money-making-systems/-systems/

Join us on Social Media:
Facebook: http://www.facebook.com/dccordova
http://www.facebook.com/moneyandyou

Twitter: http://www.Twitter.com/MoneyandYou
http://www.Twitter.com/DCCordova

Listen to http://www.MoneyandYouRadio.com – a series of audio interviews with Money & You Notable Grads and friends that will inspire and educate you

Educational videos about key principles from Money & You Program:
http://www.moneyandyou.com/rulesofthegamevideo/
http://www.moneyandyou.com/myfreegift/
https://plus.google.com/u/0/events/c3skr1ueqh134thl1n8qk6qilfg
https://www.youtube.com/watch?v=F-4BOIFrD0E
More found on YouTube: Dame DC Cordova / Money & You

Renewable energy global endeavors. Check out our partner **Huang Ming,** one of the world's leading Sustainability Entrepreneur: http://www.SolarValleyChina.com

Education / Top-level Network of the renewable energy industry: http://www.areday.net

DISC Personality Profiles:
Carol Dysart and Sandra Davis – DISC Masters of Money & You®
http://www.peoplesmartworld.com/disc-reports.html
Contact Carol@Excellerated.com with your questions or requests to use DISC in your own work or become certified as a PeopleSmart Method™ consultant.

The Family Bank Game / ACHIEVEST:
This organization is committed to helping end the cycle of generational poverty and create a new cycle of generational wealth using the decentralized financial model and community:
http://www.TheFamilyBankGame.com
See financial literacy educational video about Family Bank Game:
https://www.youtube.com/watch?v=2QGTlFLaQPE

Global Energy projects based on Dr. R. Buckminster Fuller's highest priority:
http://www.GENI.org   http://www.wrsc.org

Educational videos of Dr. R. Buckminster Fuller's principles:
www.FullerEducation.org

Planning System and Program – PERT
http://www.planinparadise.com/ppi_home.htm

Masterful Business and Personal Coaching:
http://www.accomplishmentcoaching.com

Excellent Online Marketing Strategy – Dwain Jeworski – DB Marketing Group
DwainJeworski@gmail.com

Sales Training with extraordinary systems by Sales Master:
http://www.saleschampion.com/eric-lofholm/

Web TV – Access to Expert TV looking for Guest Experts
Free training videos: http://accesstoexperts.tv

Excellent Web Support Services – DreamWarrior
http://www.dreamwarrior.com

International Business Attorney – Expert in China:
http://www.polinlawfirm.com

Intellectual Property, Internet Law, Trademark & Copyrights Expert Attorney:
http://www.jaburgwilk.com/our-people/maria-crimi-speth

Financial and Multi-Generational Estate Planning:
Expert with 30 years of planning experience:
bobryan.cfp.chfc.clu@gmail.com

Liberation Breathing:
Conscious connected breathing that restores your mind / body to health & wellness: http://www.SondraRay.com

Lindwall Releasing Method:
Deep transformational processes to release patterns or negative programs in subconscious mind: Www.thepowerofreleasing.com

Please support these awesome non-profit projects created by
Money & You® **graduates and friends:**

www.8keys.org
http://www.newhorizons-sfv.org
www.samaritanspurse.org/what-we-do/operation-christmas-child/
http://www.tummiesmindsspirits.com
www.DifferenceMakersInternational.org
http://createglobalhealing.org
http://www.WhiteRoseYouth.org
http://www.LifeTracks.org
www.pachamama.org
jennadruckcenter.org
www.NetworkVisions.org
www.globaldentalrelief.org
www.IPTforCancer.com
http://cure4hunger.org

If you wish for your organization to be included:
info@moneyandyou.com

We have been making a difference through transformational, experiential, entrepreneurial education and "churning out" Social Entrepreneurs for nearly 4 decades! The tools, exercises, and resources mentioned in this Series have allowed us to create a legacy that will last for centuries.

If you are in alignment with our work, we'd love to hear from you and learn more about your projects, organizations, and your legacy.

May your life be filled with success – both personal and business – health, joy, peace, prosperity and contribution for the betterment of humanity!

Aloha, Dame DC Cordova
http://www.MoneyandYou.com
E-mail: info@moneyandyou.com Phone: + 1-619-224-8880

Testimonials About the Work
(Continued)

"My husband John and I had just set up our own law firm, and I'd heard such good reports about M&Y that I asked him to join me to attend the programme to explore the nuts and bolts of running our own business. Neither of us was prepared for the life-changing experience which is the essence of M&Y. This programme lifted us up, shook up all of our limiting beliefs, opened our eyes, turned us upside down and then put us back gently to begin a whole new journey of self-discovery. We immediately introduced the business principles which we'd learned at M&Y into our new law firm, and they are the core values of our firm to this very day, over 22 years along the track. We also experienced huge personal benefits from M&Y, because we learned a whole new language of communication which has allowed us to become very clear with each other, both as business partners and as husband and wife. We put both of our daughters through M&Y and this took our family life to a whole new level. Once the principles and language of M&Y have been learned and applied, there is no going back. Everything in life takes off to reveal a magnificent brightness of the future."

Di Butler – Strategic Planning Team – Butler Barristers & Solicitors

"I attended Money & You when I was just 23 years young. For me, it became a pivotal experience that laid the foundation for my future as a person and, as an entrepreneur. I used what I learned to produce incredible results across my whole career. Results ranging from establishing my first business at 23, with just $1,100 and no ability to get credit, to successfully selling that business for 6 figures just 4 years later. Later establishing a non profit foundation, stepUP and inspired some 19,000 underprivileged teens. On to founding a coaching and consulting space with 65 Franchisees all making a difference to the SME market in Australia and New Zealand. To now in my role as a Group CEO of a $100M construction company; putting my entire leadership team through Money & You to create a stronger culture of personal responsibility, cooperation, synergy, communication and a focus on win:win:win results. No matter which enterprise, the distinctions of Money & You are literally part of who I am and have been in business throughout. I am and will be forever and profoundly grateful for the education this program provided me at the start of my working life – it has been a gift."

Ryll Burge-Doyle – Group CEO, Unita Group

"Over the past 20 years I have built a business which has turned over approaching $200 million dollars of products in the anti-aging and wellness industry. I registered for the program out of curiosity — not really thinking there was much I could learn in a short 3 1/2 day program. Well was I wrong!! During the program I identified a number of blindspots which I had never seen before. Post Money & You I have implemented a number of processes and systems which have seen my business become much less hands on and leveraged in short more profitable with less time. I am certain that over the next 24 months our business which has taken 20 years to build will double. If you are like me and ore than a little skeptical, then you are going to love the program."

Jeff Ghaemaghamy – Founder, ProvenPrincipels.com

"Over the past 20 years I have helped my husband build a multi-million dollar business in the anti-ageing and wellness industry, and then 5 years ago, I set out to make our money make money by investing in residential property (now a modest NZ$12 million dollar cash flow positive portfolio). After doing the Money & You program, light bulbs came on for me. I had believed we were very well leveraged in our main business, however I could see how our leverage could be even more leveraged. I cannot put into words how this program helped open up my mind to possibilities I hadn't considered, in so many different areas of my life."

Donna Ghaemaghamy – Founder, Focus On You Limited

"I have been a business owner and entrepreneur since my mid 20's - established, bought and sold businesses in Australia and New Zealand. Doing this program in 2015 really made a difference to the context in which I operate in my business and personal life. I could see how to take my next venture and my self personally to a whole new level of success and contribution. The shift in results was so significant that my wife and I plus 2 friends bought the rights to deliver the programs in Australia and New Zealand. Whether you are in business, looking at starting a business or as an employee looking for personal growth and leadership, this program definitely delivers."

Craig Doyle – Founder, Burgin and Doyle Group

"As a housewife exploring entrepreneurship, in Singapore, I was very inspired attending Money & You, in Chinese, in Oct. 2002. Within 2 months of attending the program, I launched one business idea that I got at the program that fetched me an ROI of more than 100% of my investment to Money & You, in 8hours! It was a huge self-esteem booster. Life has never been the same again. One of the greatest reward has been the global community of like-minded friends, who further inspired me to do soul-searching and live my purpose."
Azeeza Jalaludeen – Co-Founder, SHINE Group of Co.'s

"Money & You has been a powerful instrument in aligning my business teams and global partnerships. It demonstrates the most important element for successful organisations and conscious global leaders, of the 21st Century: collaboration!"
Dr AR Ramesh Nambiar – Co-Founder, SHINE Group of Co.'s

"To me living the Money & You principles means to love comprehensively, no matter where we are from. The experiential games and learnings in the program makes it possible for us to connect at deeper levels and support each other in life."
Simon Lim Geok Boon – Business Strategist & CFO of SHINE Group of Companies. Director, Armstrong Capitals Sdn Bhd

"In 1981 Money & You changed the course of my life. I had recently left the Air Force as a Captain and started my first company. I was doing well and had many clients. Money & You awakened me to expansive possibilities that I could not previously see; opportunities to contribute to the evolution of humanity and create a legacy lasting far beyond the life of one person or company."
Glenn Head – Conscious Leadership Coach, Author

"Money & You transformed and expanded me from a successful, left-brained, should-driven workaholic U.S. Senate staffer to a more fully integrated creative expression of love. Since learning and applying Money & You principles, I have created a multi-million dollar business; enjoy great relationships with friends, family and business associates in three stellar home locations; and published four books to guide others to enjoy life while making their unique contribution to the good of the whole."
Marian Head – Author, Revolutionary Agreements and Gratitude Journal for a Healthy Marriage

"30 years ago we both - by sheer chance - attended the same Money & You in Melbourne Australia... and our lives changed forever! The nurse and the accountant became global entrepreneurs and everything we have done has been touched by the lifelong learning we gained from this program."
**Jane & Stan Jordan – Intl Business Coaches/Mentors
Real Estate Investors**

"As CEO of Women Network and President of the California Women's Conference, I have the honor of attending events all around the world and Money & You was one of the most transformational experiences to date, for both my daughter and I, as it relates to my relationship with money, which prior to the conference was challenged. Dame DC Cordova has been a light for so many who struggle with their ability to have a thriving relationship with money. The timing of the conference helped navigate me through my first year producing the largest running conference globally for women...thank you!"
Michelle Patterson – CEO, Women Network & California Women's Conference

"From the opening remarks to the last moment, this was the most comprehensive, all encompassing, difficult, and heartfelt experience on money and self that I've ever had!"
Char Ravelo – Leadership Kauai Executive Director

"It engaged the brain and the heart to work together in bringing about a new level of awareness on my relationship with money. It's life-changing!"
Kaluna Wong – Leadership Kauai Office Support

"One of the most significant training events I have ever done is Money & You! I regularly use the principles I learned at that training to this day. Attend! You will love it like I did!"
Eric Lofholm – Best Selling author of *The System*

"I was able to immediately start implementing some of the techniques. This had a dramatic effect not only on our profitability but also on the harmony with which tasks were done."
Kevin Bailey – Regional Manager, Monitor Money

"I woke up and realized I could do whatever I wanted to do in my life. Started a publishing company and have published 200 books as a result 20 years later. So it was an incredible experience."
Carol Holand – Business Owner

"I personally believe that if I had attended Money & You program 7 or 8 years ago, I would have given Mark Zuckerberg, a run for his money in becoming the youngest billionaire! The program has taught me the value of money and the power of me, unleashed."
Vinod Kumar – CEO and Founder, Space Trek Global

"If you want a Millionaire Mindset, you must attend Money & You. I did and it was fantastic."
Gerry Robert – Bestselling author – The Millionaire Mindset

"Money & You may not have made me a millionaire overnight, but it has made me richer in so many aspects of my life - both in the office and at home. I am implementing cost-effective systems to promote greater efficiently and a positive environment. I recommend Money & You to all those who wants to realize and push beyond their own potential."
Julie Sherborn, Editor-in-Chief, Elle Magazine

"I was able to immediately start implementing some of the techniques. This had a dramatic effect not only on our profitability but also on the harmony with which tasks were done."
Kevin Bailey, Regional Manager – Monitor Money

"Money & You is the most transformational program I have experienced. The principles I learned have transformed the way I see myself, my business and the world around me. I've learned what my natural strengths are, which makes it so much easier to interact with business associates, clients and my family. My business is growing exponentially and designed to support the rapid growth in the global marketplace. Plus, I have incorporated a 'do good' component into every project we take on. Now I live my life according to my definition of success and that's what I call freedom."
Ann DeVere – Executive Producer, Access To Experts

"What I got from my favorite course ever, Money & You, is that it has a lifetime impact. I still remember, and use, the tools, distinctions and insights I got about myself from my very first event... WAY back in 1980! My global network is expansive and I have access to contacts and wealth everywhere I go!"

Carol Dysart, M.S. Counseling – DISC Profiles Expert

"I attended M&Y over 10 years ago. I had known about it for several years but just didn't think it was worth the investment of time and money. A decade later and there is not a day that I have doubted the value of the program. While it had a huge affect in the short time, it continues to this day to influence the way I conduct business, at all levels. So many programs come and go – Money & You has endured the changes in time, economy and generations."

Dr. Serge Gravelle – Chairman, DePan Media
Director, FEA (Foundation for Equestrian Athletes)

"Without attending Money & You, I would not have the courage to quit my paid jobs to open my own business. I resigned from the jobs I had worked for more than 20 years, two weeks after I attended the seminar. Now I own a million-dollar business. I could not believe it. But it is happening to me. This is the most brilliant program that I've ever attended. It[s worth more than the money I spent. It changed me and my life."

Nuon So Thero – President, THEROEXPRESS, Cambodia

"My experience of Money & You was that it provided an inner awakening within individuals of the true purpose of business and making lots of money. It demonstrated that money was an energetic expression of our innate will, love and power. And it provided the practical tools and understanding for achieving real success in business, making money, prosperity, abundance and happiness."

Anatole Petrovich Konnewsky – Composer, Filmmaker, Author and Entrepreneur

"I took the Money & You course in 1980, and the core understanding of these generalized principles applied to small businesses have stayed with me ever since. M&Y offered a new toolbox to use in my life and work, enabling a deeper commitment to making a difference locally and globally. You can go anywhere in the world and connect with the Money & You family of graduates."

Peter Meisen – President Global Energy Network Institute (GENI.org)

Any questions? admin@MoneyandYou.com

To learn more about the tools, processes and exercises mentioned in this publication and bonus packs:

http://www.MoneyandYou.com/Book

We welcome your feedback, inquiries, comments and suggestions!

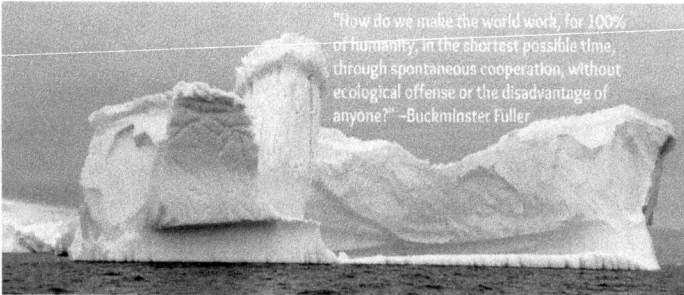

"How do we make the world work, for 100% of humanity, in the shortest possible time, through spontaneous cooperation, without ecological offense or the disadvantage of anyone?" –Buckminster Fuller

www.ingramcontent.com/pod-product-compliance
Lightning Source LLC
Chambersburg PA
CBHW070939210326
41520CB00021B/6972